Didier LODIEU

III. Pz. Korps at
KURSK

THE PART PLAYED BY 6. PZ. DIV., 7. PZ., 19. PZ. DIV. AND S. PZ. ABT.503
DURING OPERATION "ZITADELLE" (CITADEL).

Translated from the French by Alan McKay

Histoire & Collections - Paris

It was thanks to reading this book about the incredible development of Operation "Zitadelle" (Citadel) that I am now able to understand better what happened in the summer of 1943.

Previously, I only had a limited "out-of-time" understanding of the details given in this book, which indeed would have been of great help when I wrote down my own impressions in the narrative "the Forgotten Soldier". The numbers and the names of the units were the job of officers; we just suffered from the results.

But for the Landsers, who were totally exhausted from fear and self-abnegation, what was needed was an additional dose of courage.

This book recounts the precision with which all the various elements of III. Pz. Korps were organised during Operation "Zitadelle", a thing which the common or garden Landser was quite ignorant of

All we had to do was get on with it...

Because of the wealth of information it contains, this book is a must for those who are interested in this period of history.

Guy Sajer

THE KURSK SALIENT

In order to reduce the Kursk salient where the Red Army was well entrenched, Hitler and his senior generals put together a pincer attack with a common objective. The first part of the pincer, comprising the 9. Armee, was to attack from the north whilst the second part was to attack from the south. The objective of the two armies and the junction point they were given, was to be the town of Kursk. The west flank of the front was to be covered by the 2. Armee, which would remain in its positions and prevent any Russian breakthrough.

Responsibility for the south pincer fell to Generalfeldmarschall Von Manstein, one of the greatest strategists in the German army. His forces, spread out in Heeresgruppe South, comprised two armies: the 4. Pz. Armee and the Armee Abteilung Kempf. The 4. Pz. Armee regrouped three-quarters of the armoured units assigned to Heeresgruppe South. The strength of these two armies totalled 331 907 soldiers and 1 508 Panzers without counting the supporting materiel.

When the offensive was launched on 5 July 1943, the two armies in Heeresgruppe South were faced with Russian units entrenched in positions which they had already been preparing for several months. The German troops did not know what was waiting for them but they were aware that the Russians had the advantage of the terrain and a large arsenal. However, what OKW really did not know was to what extent the Russians were prepared, and what sort of welcome they would be giving the Germans.

Above: *Generalfeldmarschall von Manstein studying the map of the front with several senior officers. Among them are Generaloberst Karl Adolf Hollidt, Kdr. of the 6. Armee (from 5 March 1943) and Gen. d. Pz. Tr., Kempf, Kdr of the Armee Abteilung Kempf.* (BA22/2927/26)

The last dispositions concerning the attack against Kursk have been made, with Generalfeldmarschall von Manstein seen here on the left. He is with Generaloberst Kempf, Kdr. of the Armee Abteilung Kempf and Generalleutnant Werner Forst, Kdr. of the 16.I.D. which was responsible to the XI.A.K. (BA 22/2927/30)

A column of SU 76s moving behind the Russian 7th Army's front. This army had two regiments of tank-busters kept in reserve in case III. Pz. Korps broke through its lines of defence. (Dr Caption by M. Chaubiron)

THE ROLE OF III. PZ. KORPS WITHIN ARMY GROUP SOUTH

Although 4. Pz. Armee, with its II. SS-Pz. Korps and XXXXVIII. Pz. Korps, was the spearhead of Army Group South, Armee Abteilung Kempf nonetheless played a determining role in this vast operation.

III. Pz. Korps, under General der Panzertruppen (Gen.d.Pz. Tr.) Breith, supported by XXXII. and XI A.K. made up of infantry divisions, was its only armoured corps and had to break-through the lines of defence in order to advance northwards. Its mission was to establish an obstacle against which Russian reinforcements would exhaust themselves. This obstacle would enable the II. SS-Pz. Korps of 4. Pz. Armee, situated on the east wing of III. Pz. Korps, to reach Kursk directly.

III. Pz. Korps under Gen. d. Pz. Tr. Breith, with its 6. Pz. Div., 7. Pz. Div. and 19. Pz. Div., was to play a very important part in the way operations developed. As with all German armoured divisions, these three big units were thought of as the Heer's elite units.

To increase their firepower, each of them was reinforced by one of the three companies of s. Pz. Abt. 503, equipped throughout with the new 58-tonne Tiger

tank. The battalion's strength consisted of 45 of these machines, representing 15% of this army corps'strength - exactly 310 tanks according to the Gliederungen (rolls). To this were added 158 Sturmgeschütze, of which 31 were assigned to Stug. Abt.228, totalling in all 468 tanks. According to other sources, III. Pz. Korps had between 375 and 419 tanks. To be precise, 200 artillery pieces from Art. Rgt.612 and s. Haub. Abt. 857 (21 cm) have to be added to the 54 rocket-launchers from Werfer-Regiment 54 and the AA guns from Flak Regiment 153 which arrived in the Belgorod sector on 1 July.

Although these figures might seem high, they are comparable to those of the 25th Corps of the 70th Army of the Guard, which III. Pz. Korps was going to be fighting.

In order to cover its 10 km (6 miles) front - the exact width of the III. Pz. Korps attack zone - this Russian corps

disposed of the 78th and 81st Infantry Divisions. The latter was reinforced by the 262nd Armoured Regiment. A third infantry division, the 73rd, itself reinforced by the 176th Armoured Regiment, was placed in the second line. In case III. Pz. Korps broke through its lines of defence, the Russian 7th Army could throw in two tank brigades (224

FORCES USED BY III. PZ. KORPS DURING OPERATION "ZITADELLE" (CITADEL):	
- 6. Pz. Div.	- Werfer-Rgt. 54
- 7. Pz. Div.	- Pi. Rgt. 601 (mot.)
- 9. Pz. Div.	- Pi. Rgt. 674
- 168. I.D.	(Stab., mot.)
- s. Pz. Abt. 503	- Pi. Btl. 70 (mot.)
- Arko 3	- Pi. Btl. 651 (mot.)
- Art. Rgt.	- Pi. Btl. 127
- s. Haub. Abt. 857	(mot. 2. Kp)
(21 cm)	- Bau-Btl. 531
- II./Art. Btl. 62	- Bau-Btl. 925
- II./s. Art. Btl. 71	- Flak Regiment 99
- Stug. Abt. 228	- Flak Regiment 153.

6. PZ. DIV.'S ORGANISATION

Kdr. of the division: Generalmajor von Hünersdorff

Ia: Hauptmann Weise

Pz. Rgt. 11 (103 tanks): Oberst Hermann von Oppeln Bronikowski
This regiment only had one Abteilung: II./Pz. Rgt. 11 commanded by Major Dr Bäke

Headquarters:
- 6 Pz. II (2 cm)
- 7 Pz. III (5 cm)
- 8 Pz. III (75-mm)

5. Kp.: Oberleutnant Schöner (replaced by Lt Huchtmann)
- 4 Pz. III (75-mm)
- 6 Pz. IV (75-mm)
- 10 Pz. III (5 cm)

6. Kp.:
- 4 Pz. III (75-mm)
- 7 Pz. IV (75-mm)
- 8 Pz. III (75-mm)

7. Kp.: Oberleutnant Reutemann
- 4 Pz. III (75-mm)
- 8 Pz. IV (75-mm)
- 7 Pz. III (5 cm)

8. Kp.: Oberleutnant Spiekermann
- 3 Pz. III (75-mm)
- 8 Pz. IV (75-mm)
- 13 Flammpanzers
- 9 Pz. III (5 cm)

Pz. Gren. Rgt.4: Oberst Unrein
Pz. Gren. Rgt.114: Major Rogalla Constantin von Bieberstein
I. Btl.: Hauptmann Oeckel
II. Btl.: Hauptmann Necknauer
Pz. Art. Rgt.76: Oberstleutnant Alexander von Grundherr
Pz. AA. 6: Hauptmann Friedrich Quentin
Pz. Pi. Btl.57: Major Wolf? (He was in command of this battalion in December 1942)
Pz. Nachr. Abt. 82: Oberstleutnant Horst Moll
Heeres-Flak-Art.-Abt. 298: Hauptmann Hermann Ziegler
Pz. Jg. Abt. 41: Hauptmann Daniel Neckenauer

Divisional insignia for 6. Pz. Div. during the Battle of Kursk.

General der Panzertruppen Hermann Breith commanded III. Pz. Korps during Operation Citadel. He was 51 and a WWI veteran; he rapidly quit the infantry to join the tank arm. It was thus that in September 1939, he was in command of the armoured division of the 4. Pz. Armee. Six months later he was at the head of the 5. Pz. Brigade, then of the famous 3. Pz. Div. which made such dazzling advances in the Caucasus. He was then appointed to command III. Pz. Korps during the Battle of Kursk. General Breith was captured on the last day of the war. He died in 1964.
(Photo J. Charita. Coll. D.L.)

Right.
Gen. d. Pz. Tr. Breith studying the battlefield with Generalfeldmarschall von Manstein.
(Photo: J. Charita. Coll.: D.L.)

tanks and 22 assault guns), three regiments of tanks and two regiments of tank-busters. On the other side, Gen. d. Pz. Tr. Breith had no reserves at all…

Moreover, in order to cover the 7th Army's front, facing Armee-Abteilung Kempf, M.S. Shumilov had 27 solidly dug-in anti-tank positions with 290 heavy guns (against 317 on the German side), 506 anti-tank guns, 777 82-mm and 120-mm mortars, and 47 Katyushas.

In addition to this deployment of forces, there was a third line of defence, made up of the 89th Infantry division which could be backed up by 168 tanks from the 2nd Guard's Armoured Corps. This latter corps, with the other four armoured corps, were from the Voronesh front reserves – a total force of 1 011 tanks.

When one looks at where each German armoured corps in Heeersgruppe South was placed, it is clear that III. Pz. Korps was at a disadvantage

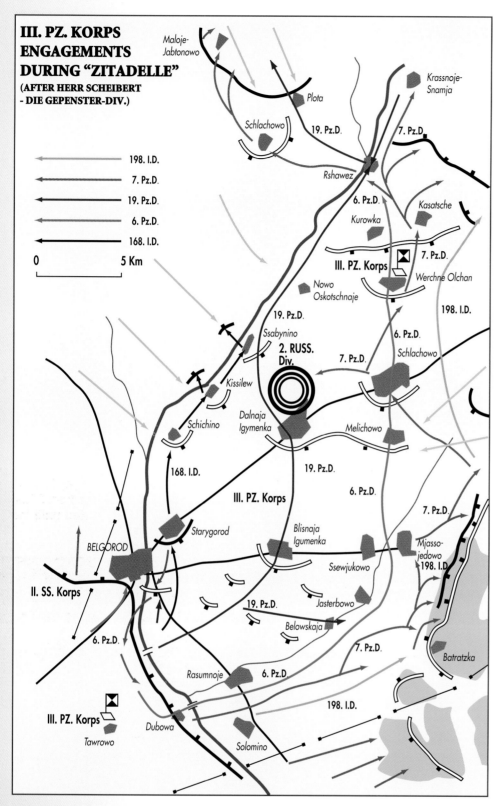

III. PZ. KORPS ENGAGEMENTS DURING "ZITADELLE"

(AFTER HERR SCHEIBERT - DIE GEPENSTER-DIV.)

198. I.D.
7. Pz.D.
19. Pz.D.
6. Pz.D.
168. I.D.

0   5 Km

Maloje-Jabtonowo
Plota
Schlachowo
19. Pz.D.
7. Pz.D.
Krassnoje-Snamja
Rshawez
6. Pz.D.
Kurowka
Kasatsche
III. PZ. KORPS
7. Pz.D.
Werchne Olchan
Nowo Oskotschnaje
198. I.D.
19. Pz.D.
6. Pz.D.
Ssabynino
2. RUSS. Div.
7. Pz.D.
Schlachowo
Kissilew
Schichino
Dalnaja Igymenka
Melichowo
168. I.D.
19. Pz.D.
6. Pz.D.
III. PZ. KORPS
7. Pz.D.
Starygorod
Blisnaja Igumenka
Mjasso-jedowo
198. I.D.
BELGOROD
Ssewjukowo
II. SS. Korps
19. Pz.D.
Jasterbowo
Belowskaja
6. Pz.D.
7. Pz.D.
Batratzka
III. PZ. KORPS
Rasumnoje
6. Pz.D.
Tawrowo
Dubowa
198. I.D.
Solomino

---

compared with XXXXVIII Pz. Korps and II. SS-Pz. Korps, placed further north. Indeed once the offensive was launched, compared to II. SS-Pz. Korps whose east flank it had to protect, III. Pz. Korps had to close up a six-mile gap. This handicap could be exploited by the Russians who could breach the line at the point the two German army corps joined.

III. Pz. Korps had to advance very quickly in the direction of Skorodnzhe, situated about 100 miles to the southeast of Kursk, to make sure that II. SS-Pz. Korps'east flank was protected. It is worth noting that Skorodnzhe is 55 miles from Belgorod, a town situated on 6. Pz. Div.'s departure point.

6. Pz. Div.'s line of departure ran along

Left:
General der Panzertruppen Werner Kempf, Kdr. of the Armee-Abteilung Kempf arriving in XXXXVIII Pz. Korps'sector of 4. Pz. Armee with one of the corps commanders, Generaloberst Raus of XI. A. K. Apart from this infantry corps, Kempf also had III. Pz. Korps and XXXXII A.K. under his command. The triangular flag held by the NCO on the left shows that Kempf is visiting an infantry battalion, probably from 167 I.D., the only infantry division in the XXXXVIII Pz. Korps. Note that this NCO has the higher gorget worn especially by standard-bearers.
(© ECPAD KBZ NUF 184406)

the west bank of the Donets, from Pokrovka to the southeast of Solomino. Gen. d. Pz. Tr. Breith's main worry was to get his Panzertruppen across the river without attracting the Russians'attention. He thought he had solved the problem by sending Luftwaffe aircraft flying over the zone his corps was going to attack. The idea was confirmed and from the night of 1 to 2 July two Junkers Ju 52 flew over the sector chosen for his tanks.

Moreover, getting 6. and 19. Pz. Div. ready had to be done during the night of 4 to 5 July. This was tedious work needing a skilled organiser. Gen. d. Pz. Tr. Breith entrusted Hauptmann von Kageneck, Kdr. of s. Pz. Abt. 503, with this task. He went to the fork in the road at Puschkarnozhe North, in order to supervise 6. Pz. Div. and 19. Pz. Div. crossing the bridges to the north and to the south of Mikhailovka respectively.

Although he was forewarned of the date and time of the start of the German offensive, General Watutin, the Russian Commander-in-Chief of the Voronesh front, was worried by the presence of the German armoured forces. II. SS-Pz. Korps and III. Pz. Korps meant no less than six armoured divisions concentrated along a front of 18 to 25 miles. There was a great risk of them overwhelming a large stretch of his first line of defence.

As a result Watutin had all the artillery units of the 6th Guards Army to open fire on the German positions from 22.30 onwards. The barrage lasted until the offensive was launched.

19. PZ. DIV. ORGANISATION

Kdr. of the Division: Generalleutnant Gustav Schmidt
Pz. Rgt. 27: Oberst Heinrich Becker
1 Befehl (Command) Pz. IIIs – 1 Befehl Pz. III (l.) - 1 Pz. III (5)

I./Pz. Rgt. 27:
    1 Pz. III (l.) – 1 Pz. III (kz.) – 1 Pz. III (75)
1.Kp.: 5 Pz. IIIs (l.) – 3 Pz. IIIs (5)
2.Kp.: 5 Pz. IIIs (l.) - 3 Pz. IIIs (5)
3.Kp.: 9 Pz. IVs (l.)
4.Kp.: 9 Pz. IVs (l.) – 2 Pz. IVs (kz)

II./Pz. Rgt. 27:
2 Befehl Pz. IIIs – 5 Pz. IIIs (l.) – 1 Pz. III (kz)
5. Kp.: 5 Pz. IIIs (lg.) – 3 Pz. IIIs (75)
6. Kp.: 9 Pz. IVs (l.)
7. Kp.: 9 Pz. IVs (l.)
This armoured regiment comprised
    2 Pz. IIs
    38 Pz. IIIs
    38 Pz. IVs
    3 Befehl Pzs.
Pz. Gren. Rgt. 73: Oberst Rudolf Köhler replaced by Major Horst on 6 July
Pz. Gren. Rgt. 74: Kdr.: Oberstleutnant Helmut Richter
Pz. Art. Rgt. 19: Oberstleutnant Karl Goernemann
Pz. Pi. Btl. 19: Major Gerhard Nemnich
Pz. Nachr. Abt. 19: Hauptmann Franz-Josef Vacano
Pz. AA. 19: Major Wilmsen
Heeres-Flak. Abt 272: Hauptmann Frhr. Von Hohenhausen
Pz. Jg. Abt. 19:
Stug. Abteilung 228: Hauptmann Malachowski

Documentary report with s. Pz. Abt. 503
by Bild Berichter Wolf-Alvater from PK 637
(Propaganda Company N°637. – DAT 3021)

s. Pz. Abt. 503

During Operation Citadel, this battalion's three companies equipped with 45 Tiger tanks were engaged separately and each attached to one of III. Pz. Korps' armoured regiments. The 1. Kp. was attached to 6. Pz. Div., the 2. Kp. to 19. Pz. Div. and the 3. Kp. to 7. Pz. Div. Their role was to cover the Panzer IIs, IIIs and IVs whose armour was very much thinner than the Tiger's. During small scale operations, the Tigers protected the light tanks following the attack. Here Tiger 123 can be seen in the Generalovka sector. The crew is relaxing while ammunition is being replenished.
(BA 22/2949/5)

The Kdr. of s. Pz. Abt. 503, Hauptmann Clemens Graf von Kageneck says in his biography: "I was born on 17 October 1913. My father was Military Attaché in Brussels then in Vienna. He also served in the Hussars at Potsdam and finished WWI commanding a brigade with the rank of General (…)

Our family was totally opposed to Adolf Hitler and his Nazi Party in 1933. At the end of 1931, I started studying law at Freiburg-Bonn. My studies were interrupted in the third semester by my period of military service with the Reiter Regiment 4 which became Pz. Rgt.6.

At the beginning of 1939, I took part in the march on Prague, one of the easiest stages of the war. In September 1939, I was a Leutnant and in command of a platoon of five Pz. Is. On 2 September, my tank was hit by an anti-tank shell and my driver killed.

I fought for almost three weeks during the Polish campaign. I was awarded the Iron Cross, Second class. During the Battle of France in 1940, I was a Signals Officer (Nachtrichtenoffizier) with II./Pz. Rgt. 6. In 1941, I was Pz. Rgt. 6's Signals officer.

Left: *Hauptmann Clemens Graf von Kageneck*
(BA 183-R64039)

We were engaged during that horrible winter near Moscow. I was awarded the Iron Cross, First Class, near Orel.

In March 1942, I became the CO of 4./ Pz. Rgt. 6 during the campaign in the Caucasus for which I was awarded the German Gold Cross.

In October 1941, I was the first ordnance officer to the 3.Pz. Div. After the defeat at Stalingrad, I fought during the retreat. From April to June 1943, I went on a course for Battalion Commanding Officers at Putlos and Paris.

On 10 May 1943, I took command of s. Pz. Abt. 503 with the rank of Hauptmann. It was thanks to Gen. d. Pz. Tr. Breith, the former Kdr. of 3. Pz. Div. under whom I had served during the battles in the Caucasus, that I was given this post. When I arrived in Karkhov, the Abteilung was ready with its 45 Tigers.

Oberst Hoheisel who had been CO of s. Pz. Abt. 503 since 25 January 1943, handed over command of the Abteilung in June 1943.

After two weeks of violent fighting, I was seriously wounded. I was then evacuated to Germany where I remained for eight weeks convalescing. In recognition of the Abteilung's success during Operation Citadel, I was awarded the Knight's Cross on 5 August 1943.

I returned to the Abteilung at the end of 1943. It was with Army Group South that the 503rd fought during the very difficult withdrawal which reached its paroxysm with the crossing of the Dniepr in December.

At the beginning of January 1944, we were engaged in the defensive fighting to the west of Kiev and in the south of the Ukraine.

On 24 January we were ordered by General Hübe to join Panzergruppe Bäke in order to try and open up the Tcherkassy pocket. On 30 January 1944 I was wounded for the fourth time. In recognition of s. Pz. Abt. 503's success, I was awarded the Oak Leaves which I added to my Knight's Cross.

"In December 1944, I took over command of the tank training school at Bergen which remained unprotected until the end of the war."

After captivity, Clemens Graf von Kageneck became a bank manager then chief executive of the Hardy Bank of Berlin - Frankfurt in 1962. He retired in 1978 and died in2004.

Middle:
During the summer of 1943, the Tiger became a legend. War correspondents and propaganda agents followed the units using these formidable tanks mile after mile. This one has just opened fired on Russian tanks from 1 600 yards. It is impossible to say whether they have been hit but they most certainly could have been, the maximum range of the 88-mm gun being 1_ miles. The Tiger's shot was probably guided by the observer hiding in the large foxhole (in line with the barrel). Only his head is sticking out. Note the headphones placed on the ground. There is another Tiger to the right of his position and the outline of a Panzer IV coming back to friendly positions can just be made out on the far right.
(© ECPAD DAT 3021 - L 9)

Left:
Crews concerting; they have to get more information before carrying on and firing; they have to save on petrol and shells. Indeed during training, the Panzerschützen learned that one week's work was needed by one worker to make a shell and that another person had to provide 100 RM to finance its production. Firing the machine gun instead of the 88-mm gun was recommended
(© ECPAD DAT 3021 - L 15)

The Petlyakov Pe-2 was an elegant twin-engined dive-bomber produced from June 1940 onwards; it was often nicknamed the "Soviet Mosquito" because it was capable of competing with the German Me 109 fighters owing to its speed and manoeuvrability. (DR - Caption by M. Chaubiron)

THE FIRST DAY OF THE OFFENSIVE: 5 JULY 1943

On 5 July, the three armoured divisions of the III. Pz. Korps got under way under a deluge of steel and fire showered down on it by the Russian artillery. They overtook part of the troops from Generalmajor Chales de Beaulieu's 168 I.D. who held the west bank of the Donets – they had been reinforced by the I./Pz. Gren. Rgt 7 during the night of the 3rd to 4th – then they got ready to go into action on the east flank of the armoured corps. The III. Pz. Korps artillery had used up all its ammunition on enemy targets since that same night (3rd-4th July): for instance, the Kanoniere of Art. Rgt. 248 had not hesitated to shoot off 1 325 shells in order to destroy two Russian batteries on the eve of the offensive. Alas, the XI.A.K. positioned on the east wing of the armoured corps did not give the support that was expected: its two infantry divisions, preceded by two Abteilungen of assault cannon came under fire of the Russian 7th Army's artillery!

This unexpected barrage prevented III. Pz. Korps from crossing the river rapidly. Its Panzerdivisions (6., 7. And 19. Pz. Div.) encountered a number of difficulties and the three companies of Tigers of s. Pz. Abt. 503, which opened the way for them were the first to suffer casualties.

THE 6. PZ. DIV. SECTOR

Placed to the north of the armoured army corps under Gen. d. Pz. Tr. Breith, the 6. Pz. Div. set off in an arc in front of Belgorod. Its mission was to take Staryzh Gorod and Tschernaya Polzhana. For that it had first to get through the narrow streets of Belgorod, then reach the wooden bridge at Bolchovez and cross it. The Pi. Rgt. 674 and the III./Werfer-Regiment 54 were attached to the division. Beforehand, the Kdr. of 168 I.D. had spread out most of his units to ensure the traffic was controlled and that 6. Pz. Div. was covered. The Kampfgruppe of Major Vollmary, Kdr. of Gren. Rgt. 429, which regrouped II./Gren. Rgt. 429 and II./Gren. Rgt.417, was positioned at the bridgehead, and III./Gren. Rgt. 429 was spread out along the east edge of Belgorod up to the north of Pokrova. From this zone to the left flank of the division, there was Major Barkmann's Kampfgruppe which regrouped I./Gren. Rgt. 417

and a part of the reconnaissance battalion.

Ordered to open the way for the 6. Pz. Div., the heavy Tigers from 1./s. Pz. Abt. 503 came down from the Delnazhaya Yigumenka heights to head for the bridge. The CO of the company, Hauptmann Burmester, was disappointed when he learnt that the bridge could only take a maximum load of 24 tonnes. There was no way his 58-tonne tanks could cross it. They would have to wait for the sappers from the 11th Pontoon Company to reinforce the structure of the bridge.

Under the protection of the AA guns of Flak Abt. 91 placed defensively, Oberst von Oppeln Bronikowski decided to do without of Burmester's Tigers. He ordered his light tanks to attack the 15-metre long bridge.

The Kdr of the s. Pz. Abt. 503, Hauptmann von Kageneck wrote: *"Whilst a blazing dawn was breaking in the distance, a hundred Stalin's organs launched their rockets onto the bridge, destroying the bridge very quickly. The sappers suffered heavy losses with these torpedo-like splinters, which swept across the surface of the ground.*

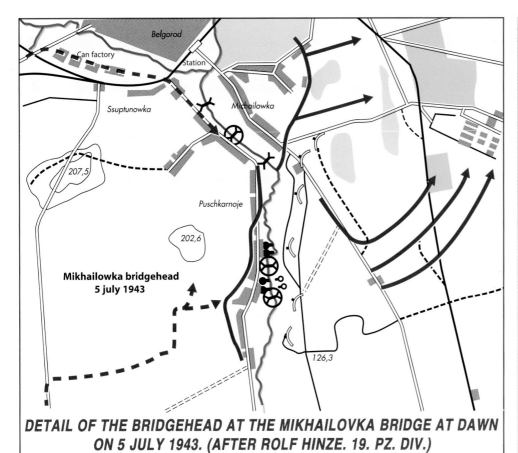

DETAIL OF THE BRIDGEHEAD AT THE MIKHAILOVKA BRIDGE AT DAWN ON 5 JULY 1943. (AFTER ROLF HINZE. 19. PZ. DIV.)

Oberstleutnant Rogalia von Bieberstein, Kdr. of the Pz. Gren. Rgt. 114. He was awarded the Knight's Cross posthumously on 24 July 1943. He was 38.
(Coll.: Josef Charita. Coll.: D.L.)

This artillery barrage showed us how crazy plans could be when they did not take into account enemy positions located on the southern slope of the bridgehead. This had to be captured since it offered a view with a range of almost one and a half miles."

The attack fell to the Panzergrenadiere of the Pz. Gren. Rgt 114 regrouped in a Kampfgruppe commanded by Oberst von Bieberstein. Like the 3./Pz. Pi. Abt. and the II./Gren. Rgt. 417 of the 168 I.D., this unit had been attached to von Oppeln Bronikowski's tactical group since the day before.

At the front, the leading units moved forward cautiously using the sides of the road, whilst the assault sappers of Pz. Pi. Abt. 57 cleared the road of mines. The 80 artillery pieces of Pz. Art. Rgt.76 under Oberstleutnant von Grundherr gave them invaluable support. Finally the Panzergrenadiere reached Staryzh Gorod station and took it. Meanwhile, Kampfgruppe Arthan (I. or II./Pz. Gren. Rgt. 114) attacked the Russian communications.

Oberstleutnant von Bieberstein thought

of continuing operations but part of his unit was missing. Indeed this was delayed because of a silly accident: an assault gun from Stug. Abt. 228 ran into a lorry from the pontoon section, on the 24 tonnes bridge at Mikhailovka. This accident was even more of a problem because it immobilised the Landsers from Gren. Rgt. 417 which ought to have been

taking part in the attack.

When Oberstleutnant von Bieberstein learnt of this, he was obliged to get his Panzergrenadiere to fall back and he set up defensive positions in the woods situated two kilometres to the northwest of Tschernaya Polzhana.

All the plans that Generalmajor von Hûnersdorf of 6. Pz. Div. and his staff had

Right

This Volkswagen Kübelwagen belongs to a motorised transport company (Kraftwagentransportkompanie). These signposts showing the location of different units would soon spread out everywhere along the roads. This car, with a top speed of 50 mph, could transport four people with their equipment. It coped perfectly well with the most difficult terrain in Russia. 55 000 were produced during the war.
(BA 22/2296/07)

Leutnant von Rosen commanded the second section of Tigers of the 3./s. Pz. Abt. 503 during the Battle of Kursk. Richard von Rosen was born in 1922. In October 1940, he was an officer cadet in Oberst Eberbach's famous Pz. Rgt. 35 which he followed into Russia during Operation Barbarossa. Promoted to Leutnant and section commander in 1942, he was transferred to the 2./s. Pz. Abt. 502 which became 3./s. Pz. Abt. 503 in January 1943. Wounded during Operation Citadel, Leutnant von Rosen rejoined his section in 1944 to take part in the Battle of Normandy. He then became commanding officer of 3./s. Pz. Abt. 503 in September 1944 and left for Hungary. After the war he joined the economic departments of several towns. He joined the German army again and became a Hauptmann in 1955. He was then employed in War Instruction GHQ, Paris. He was promoted to Generalmajor then took well-earned retirement. (Photo: von Rosen. Coll. D.L.)

made had to be revised. It was agreed that Oberst von Oppeln Bronikowski's Panzerkampfgruppe would cross the Donets at dawn in the 19. Pz. Div.'s area.

At 10.30, von Oppeln Bronikowski's armoured group crossed the bridge at Mikhailovka which could take 60 tonnes, the only one left over the Donets. Russian artillery and aircraft endeavoured to destroy the bridge and took on von Bieberstein's Kampfgruppe which was set up in its new positions. The latter had had to get along by itself because von Oppeln Bronikowski's Panzerkampf-gruppe, reinforced by an armoured section of Pioniere from the remnants of 3./Pz. Pi. Btl. 57 and II./Pz. Gren. Rgt.114, were unable to join them.

So it was without support that von Bieberstein's Kampfgruppe was ordered to attack Staryzh Gorod and it was with very heavy losses that his meagre forces captured the town at around 4 p.m.

The Kdr of the 6. Pz. Div., Generalmajor von Hünersdorff, admitted to Gen. d. Pz. Tr. Brieth of the III. Pz. Korps "...Considering the sacrifices the men of the 6.

Pz. Div. made, you can't call this a victory."

At 5 p.m., von Oppeln Bronikowski received the following order: "Your Kampfgruppe must cross the 60-tonne bridge used earlier by 7. Pz. Div. and continue the offensive".

As for Hauptmann Burmester and his first Tiger company, they were ordered

to put themselves at the disposal of Oberst von Oppeln Bronikowski's tactical group. All the armour gathered in a forest situated to the south of Kolonozh-Dubrovzh.

I./Pz. Art. Rgt.76 set off to join them. During the night of 5-6 July, part of 6. Pz. Div. was relieved and put in III. Pz. Korps'reserve. As the attack planned for that day was suspended, it was held at the disposal of the army corps in the sector of Krutozh-Log-Generalovka-Solomino. Later, it was moved to the Razumnoe sector, on both sides of Miassoyedovo. Its objective was then to reach Melikhovo.

THE 7. PZ. DIV. SECTOR

The boundary line between the 7. Pz. Div. and the 106. I.D. of the Raus Korps (XI.A.K.) was the following: Andreyevka (106 I.D.) – Solomino (7. Pz. Div.) – Uschakovo (106 I.D.) – Ploskoie (7. Pz. Div.) – Puschkamoie (7. Pz. Div.) – the river Chelk from Nikitova up to its source.

The separation between 7. Pz. Div. and the 19. Pz. Div. was: Repnoie (19. Pz. Div.) – Kolonozh-Dubrovzh (7. Pz. Div.) – Uroshaya Kolkoz (19. Pz. Div.) – Hill 215.5 to the east of Blishnaya Yigumenka (19. Pz. Div.) – the river Rasumnaya from Kalinina to it source.

The sapper section of Pz. Rgt. 25 commanded by Oberfeldwebel Baumann prepared a way through the mines for the four Tigers of the 2nd section of 3./s. Pz. Abt. 503 which had to open the way for the two other sections of 3. Kp Tigers. The CO, Leutnant von Rosen, had already come across this spot three weeks earlier. This heavy tank company

Right:
An Oberleutnant in September 1944, Richard von Rosen commanded the 3./s. Pz. Abt. 503 which was entirely re-equipped with Tiger IIs. Here is one from the 2. Kp. in the background. (Photo : von Rosen. Coll. : D.L.)

Right:
Obergefreiter and Funker Heinz Bleidiessel smoking a cigarette in the company of a comrade in front of Hauptmann Scherf's Tiger 300. The scene took place before 5 July 1943.
(Photo: H. Bleidiessel. Coll. D.L.)

had been attached to 7. Pz. Div. the day before (at 4 o'clock), as had a battery of Flak Abt. 91 to provide air protection for the bridge.

Suddenly both banks of the Donets blew up in an infernal noise and collapsed. Without wasting an instant, Oberfeldwebel Baumann fired two green cartridges with his Very pistol.

The veteran, ex-Leutnant von Rosen (now Generalmajor) wrote: *"The signal has just come: the operation was a success. Everything had been prepared in minute detail. My four crews knew down which path they had to go and where they had to wait. Panzer Marsch! (Panzer forward march)*

"Really launching off into the attack, we set out in the direction of the river. I was driving my Tiger 321 straight for the ford. Baumann told us with hand signals that all was going well. We went slowly towards the river, down the escarpment which had been all shot up by the explosions. After crossing the river Donets, we had to climb up the escarpment on the right bank.

"Because of the explosions, the earth on the bank was all churned up. The water was frothing up in front of the Panzer. Then we started to climb, but as there was no solid ground for the tank tracks to get a grip of, they started to spin. We tried a second time but to no avail. Suddenly a shower of mortar shells started to fall nearby. I radioed that the

crossing had failed. I was then ordered to remain where I was with my section. A bit later the Kdr. of the Pionier-Bataillon appeared: he had orders to build a bridge which would take 60 tonnes, protected by my Tigers because there was a risk of the Russians counter-attacking.

"To shelter my Tiger in a safe place, Feldwebel Weigl got ready to tow it with

his 324. Before that his layer, Unteroffizier Jäckel had to hook a cable to the tank's towing hook which was underwater. He managed to do this, but not without difficulty. We worked at it up to the chest in water under continuous fire from the Russians. Once the Tiger had been got out, we withdrew to the position where the bridge was to be built.

"Meanwhile, the Engineers arrived in their vehicles. The sappers needed five hours to build the bridge - a desperately long delay for the Panzergrenadiere who had to wait for the Tigers.

"The first wounded coming back from the front were loaded onto inflatable dinghies. They did not speak of us in a very friendly manner because the Russians had resisted strongly and were well organised; the two Panzergrenadiere regiments had therefore suffered heavy casualties and had barely advanced.

"The sappers worked without protection and the mortar shells went on falling.

Left:
Tiger 321 belonging to Panzerkommandant Hans Rieschel seen in the turret pausing for the photo, taken on the eve of Citadel. Rieschel was killed a year and ten days later at Emiéville in Normandy. Obergefreiter Hans Bleidiessel is on the left and Obergefreiter Willi Gehling who was wounded near Tcherkassy on 12 February 1944, is on the right.
(Photo: H. Bleidiessel. Coll. D.L.)

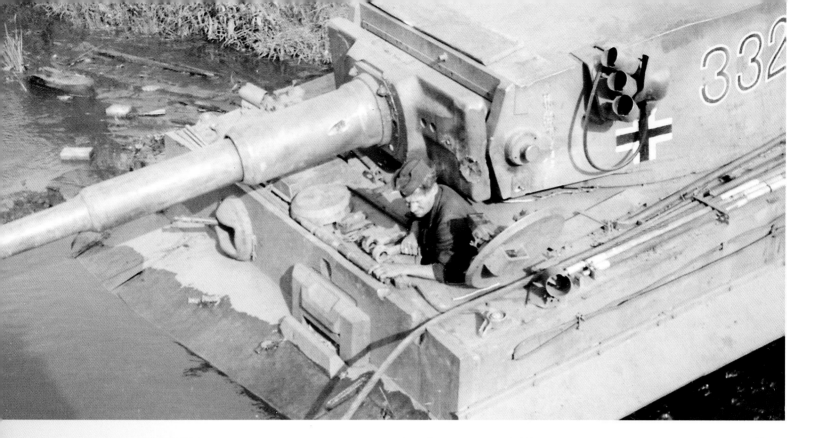

Young Leutnant von Rosen's tank found itself in a worse predicament than Tiger 332 seen here, stuck in the mud on this bank. After crossing the Donets on 5 July 1943, his tank got stuck on the bank under Russian mortar fire… During training, the crews were told not to tow a Tiger; they were to leave that to the mechanics. On the other hand, while they were waiting, if they were stuck in the mud they could free the tracks. (© ECPAD DAT 3023 L11)

Left:

On the left in Feldgrau uniform, Hauptmann Wiegand, Kdr. of the Versorgungskompanie of s. Pz. Abt. 503, talking to several officers from the Tiger battalion. On his left is Leutnant Oelmer from the 1. Kp. who subsequently commanded this company. The tallest officer is none other than Hauptmann Burmester, Kdr. of the 1. Kp., with an unknown officer.
(© ECPAD DAT 3023 L34)

Above: **Bogged down in the mud up to the hull, Tiger 332 had to be pulled out by the crew who worked relentlessly to get the towing cable free at the front of the machine.** (© ECPAD DAT 3024 L6)

Top right:
One of Tiger 321's crew seems to be bringing a track link to the crew in difficulty. (© ECPAD DAT 3024 L33)

Right:
Once the cable was freed, the Panzerschützen get ready to hook it onto the rear of their tank. It was then towed by the Tiger behind them. Tiger 332 was destroyed by mistake by a I/SS-Pz. Rgt.1 Panther on 27 January 1944. (© ECPAD DAT 3024 L7)

The waiting was unbearable. It was getting hotter. The air inside the tank was getting more and more unbreathable. We were condemned to sit still in our compartments.

"The bridge was finally ready towards 2 p.m. and we rushed towards it. Panzer Marsch! We moved up towards the terrain the Panzergrenadiere had taken during the morning."

The two Abteilungen of Pz. Rgt. 25 were separated for organisational reasons. The first, commanded directly by the HQ of the armoured regiment's Kdr., Oberstleutnant Schültz, was given the mission of attacking in depth with the support of Pz. Gren. Rgt. 7. Von Rosen's Tiger section opened up a breach for them, the objective being to build a base from which to start penetrating the Russian defences.

The second Abteilung, with 3./s. Pz. Abt. 503 (less the 2nd section) had to support Pz. Gren. Rgt. 6 which had to protect 7. Pz. Div's right flank and also, therefore, III. Pz. Korps.

Previous page bottom:
Tiger 321, belonging to Leutnant von Rosen. As they were crossing the bridge, the crew realised that it was on the brink of collapsing. So the Panzerführer (driver) took the risk, put his foot down on the accelerator and steered the tank towards the left to reach terra firma. But there was the gap between the bridge and the land and this had to be crossed. Fortunately, the 21-foot long Tiger was able to clear the obstacle. (© ECPAD DAT 3022 L12)

DOCUMENTARY REPORT ON THE 7. PZ. DIV.

Above : *Panzer IV R03 from Pz. Rgt. 25 headquarters just managing to avoid getting stuck in the mud with the help of some soldiers and Hiwis.* (BA 22/2922/3)

Below : *Wearing the black Feldmütze of the armoured units, Oberstleutnant Adalbert Schulz is also wearing a locally-made jacket cut from SS camouflage canvas. If one looks carefully, one can see the Heer's chest eagle he has sewn onto his breast to avoid possible confusion. In the background, the tactical sign of the 7. Pz. Div. worn during the Battle of Kursk.* (BA 22/2922/12)

Oberstleutnant Adalbert Schulz, Kdr of Pz. Rgt. 25, talking to one of his tank commanders during Operation Citadel. (BA 22/2922/9)

Portrait of Adalbert Schulz.
"Together with the keenness of a modern troop commander, Schulz's vivacity was a determining factor for his men, who inflicted defeat after defeat on the enemy. For them, Schulz was both a friend and a father, whose care for his soldiers knew no limits", wrote the historian Günther Fraschka. Adalbert Schulz, a Berliner, joined the police in 1925 at the age of 22. He was transferred to the armoured troops in 1935 with the rank of Oberleutnant. His first job was as CO of the 1st Company of Pz. Rgt. 25 in the 7. Pz. Div., in which he served until his last day. He quickly became CO of I./Pz. Rgt. 25 in June 1940, then the commander in chief of the regiment with the rank of Oberstleutnant three months before Operation Citadel was launched. He began 1944 with the rank of Generalmajor and commanded the 7. Pz. Div. His rise was dazzling. He was a general at only 41. But his career ended on 28 January 1944: he was hit in the head by a shell splinter. He was awarded the Knight's Cross on 29 September 1940 to which were added Oak Leaves on 31 December 1941, Epees on 6 August 1943 and Swords on 14 December 1943. (Photo J. Charita.)

Above : **By one of those lucky coincidences our colleague, Mr Charita, got hold of this shot taken by a veteran during the same period as the report from the Bundesarchiv shown here. Oberstleutnant Schulz can be seen, talking probably to one of his section commanders in 3. Kp. of Pz. Rgt. 25 - if the typical jacket cut by the battalion tailor is anything to go by. In the background, Tiger 300. On 5 July, its crew consisted of: Oberleutnant Scherf, Erwin Glas (layer), Maier (loader), Weiland (radio operator) and Wunderlich (driver)...**
(Photo J. Charita. Coll. D.L.)

Right : **"Panzer-Schulz", as his soldiers called him, sheltering behind his R01. He is showing one of his Lieutenants the objectives or the battalion positions on a map.**
(Photo J. Charita. Coll. D.L.)

Above:
The action which earned Oberstleutnant Schulz the Ritterkreuz was the one when the Russians tried to breakthrough at Kiev. He ordered the Landsers to climb onto his first battalion tanks, then together they threw themselves at the enemy's flank pushing them back. Soon after, 60 Russian tanks appeared. Keeping his head, Schulz called up his second battalion of Panzers that came to the rescue. No enemy tank got away.
(Photo J. Charita. Coll. D.L.)

Top left:
Command tank 102 of I./Pz. Rgt. 25 with its extra antenna, getting ready to leave. This is one of the three Pz. Befehlswagen mit 5 cm KwK39 L/60 from Hauptmann Fortun's headquarters, i.e. the command version of the Pz. IIIL or M. Note the rather unusual shape of the lower part of the turret shield. The tank commander - if the silver piping on his forage cap is anything to go by - must be Fortun's adjudant. The Panzerschütze in the foreground is holding what seems to be a towing hawser.
Note Tiger 300, belonging to Oberleutnant Scherf, on the right of the photo. This was lost on 11 July 1943, so this scene took place before that, probably on the eve of the offensive. During the first three days of Operation Citadel, Pz. Rgt. 25 lost 60 tanks but only seven were totally destroyed. The others were quickly repaired by the Werkstatt. On the other hand, the crew losses were heavy: the estimate was for 361 killed.
(BA 22/2922/14)

Left:
After leaving the Kdr. of the Pz. Rgt. 25, the reporter reached the Tavrovo sector where 7.Pz. Div's HQ was located together with s. Pz. Abt. 503's Werkstatt. Tavrovo was an important place because it was a part of III. Pz. Korps' supply lines. The Naschub trucks were loaded at Repnoie, then transited through Tavrovo, crossed the bridge set up by the Genie at Dorogobushinoden then they drove along the road to the east to unload the supplies to the west of Razumnoe. At Tavrovo, Oberleutnant Gross' mechanics worked night and day so that the Tigers remained operational. Top left, we can see part of the gantry under which a Tiger is being repaired. Clambering over the turret, a mechanic is handling a cable.
(BA 22/2922/19)

Left : *After fixing a cable to each side of the tank, the mechanic attaches them to a pulley suspended from the gantry.* (BA 22/2922/21)

Middle: *While the mechanics are busy with the turret, the other two seem to be removing the sprocket wheel.* (BA 22/2922/23)

Bottom left: *The mechanics start lifting the turret slowly, stabilising the mass of steel to avoid unsteadiness. In order to get at the engine, the turret had to be removed. This was one of the Tiger's major drawbacks. The work done by the workshops at the rear was indispensable; without its mechanics, an armoured unit was bound to disappear. This was why so many Panzers were lost during the Battle of Normandy.* (BA 22/2922/24)

Below : *The mechanics carefully ensure that the turret lifts off its base properly otherwise parts of the engine could be damaged or even ripped out. Note the size of the gantry: it can carry a load of 15 tonnes.* (BA 22/2922/28)

Above:
The turret is now positioned on an appropriate stand. Repair work can now start on the engine.
(BA 22/2923/7a)

Right :
This close-up enables the impressive blow that shattered part of the 110-mm gun shield armour to be seen. The missing parts have been laid out in the foreground. This turret belongs to a different Tiger from the previous one.
(BA 22/2923/13A)

by the sappers from Pi. Btl.651. It had to back up Pz. Gren. Rgt. 6, under Oberst Glaesemer, which was getting ready to attack Razumnoe.

Ex-machine-gunner and Unteroffizier Gerd Niemann from Tiger 311 recalls: *"The sun set the steel armour afire. In the compartment it was just like being in an incubator. The wounded coming back from the infantry couldn't understand why we didn't move up to the front. They cried to us again and again: 'Forward! Forward! Your comrades are waiting for you.' We finally reached the point of no-return. 'Company! March!' After a hundred yards or so, we were in contact with the enemy. 'At 2 o'clock, bunker, explosive shell.' I obeyed automatically. My foot pressed on the pedal to turn the turret, my left hand set the sights to calculate the range, then it grabbed the steering wheel to direct the canon. My right hand was ready to raise the handle. 'Identified, safety catch off! Ready to fire!' I pressed on the trigger. The target disappeared in a cloud of smoke. Did I score a hit? Leutnant Weinart did not give me time to find out. The tank was ready to move off again. Through the periscope I saw other pictures.*

"These gestures were repeated a lot of times: 'Unloaded, cloud of dust, Go!' The Tiger was constantly on the move. It swayed to the left then to the right, moved forwards or backwards. Soon I lost any sense of direction. Red Army soldiers appeared in front of our tank. We were heading straight for their defensive positions.

"Men wearing brown uniforms got up en masse to shoot at our Tiger with their rifles and sub-machine guns. Several of them retreated, others got under cover in a dip in the land. They could not stop us. Those who were not mown down by our machine guns scarpered.

"On the right there was a cereal field, the ideal place for hiding anti-tank guns. Leutnant Weinart ordered us to get rid of the enemy there. 'Direction: one o'clock. Distance: 50 metres – explosive shells – safety catch off!'

"We advanced cautiously; my forehead was stuck to the protective plate of the sights. All I could see was an ocean of wheat stalks. Suddenly a flash, then an impact hit our tank. At the same time a geyser of earth shot up some 30-40

Despite heavy Russian air activity against the attacking units, the bridgehead to the east of the Donets was firmly established and the advance units moved forward in the direction of Dalnizhe Peski and the woods to the east.

Von Rosen's section crossed the railway line near Razumnoe station. This railroad was the first Russian line of defence, where the Panzergrenadiere were halted. It was the Landsers of the 106 I.D. who finally attacked from this town.

Our veteran, ex-Leutnant von Rosen, carries on with his narrative: *"Not far from there, I went to the Pz. Gren. Rgt. 7 command post, to which I was attached when carrying out an attack. Brief instructions about the places mentioned on the map and some recommendations and we were off.*

"Leading the voltigeur companies, we engaged in violent exchanges lasting all afternoon. The Panzergrenadiere were reassured by our being there. They were worn out however by fighting Red Army soldiers buried in innumerable foxholes which they had to clear out, often fighting hand-to-hand.

"In circumstances like that we could not really help them very much. The Russians would let our Tigers go past then throw themselves on the Panzergrenadiere following. At dusk, we stocked up on petrol, ammunition and supplies brought up forward the company. Orders were transmitted during the night about the attack planned for the following day."

Meanwhile, 3./s. Pz. Abt. 503 (less the 2nd section) under Oberleutnant Scherf, ordered to open the way for II./Pz. Rgt.25, in turn crossed the 60-tonne bridge built metres into the air. 'Bravo! Bull's eye!' Only then did I realise that I had fired.

"The Tiger received other impacts. The shots came from the depths of the field, but the enemy remained invisible. Nonetheless the loader had to carry on working without wasting a moment. I followed Leutnant Weinert's instructions precisely: 'Fire again. Ivan must not get the impression he's safe.'

"A blow shook the tank. Unteroffizier Kuhnert shouted something like 'Penetration' and Obergefreiter Lehner shouted 'Wounded!' Leutnant Weinert remained totally calm: 'What else?' he asked. 'Nothing, Herr Leutnant.' 'Then let's get on, Kuhnert.'

"Calmly, like during training, Leutnant Weinert directed his Tiger across the fields towards an anti-tank gun. Left, right, left. The tracks snatched up the canon, and then broke up another one. The electrical system wasn't working any more, the humming sound in the headphones died away. Nevertheless the tank continued to move forward.

"On the right, at fifty metres, there was another anti-tank gun. The crew came round. Machine gun fire. At that moment something moved near the canon: a flash and another blow against the Tiger. Vibrations boomed inside the compartment. Before I knew what was happening, Unteroffizier Kunhert brought the barrel round into position and a fourth anti- tank gun was out of action.

"But we still weren't clear. A shot behind us stopped the engine. We stayed where we were, unable to move. The starter did not take long to start working again. I tried turning the turret by hand.

"At that moment Leutnant Weinert ordered: 'Stop!' I immediately asked: 'What happened to the anti-tank gun?' 'Oberfeldwebel Rondorf got it.' So we weren't alone. Operation 'wheat field' was drawing to an end. We were allowed to smoke a cigarette and to breathe fresh air at last.

"But things didn't stop there. Enemy tanks had been sighted. We started the engine with the crankshaft. When we left the field we ran over a mine. Fortunately our tank only suffered minor damage to the gearbox which was quickly fixed. Then we came into sight of a village (Razumnoe?). The enemy tanks were easily identifiable. Range: 1 200 metres. I only needed two shells to destroy the first tank.

"The next T-34 moved into our line of fire. It was moving fast. This time the loader needed three shells to hit it. The company settled down safely for the night."

Oberstleutnant Schulz's situation was critical; the Russian rear was bombarding his II./Pz. Rgt. 25 while it was crossing the Donets. Losses were terrible. One of his men, Arthur Scherer remembers: "The Kdr. of my Abteilung had already been wounded by a shell splinter before the attack started. He was replaced by the commander of the 6. Kp., Hauptmann Maul. This was an ominous sign.

"Our artillery let fly and the attack started. We'd hardly moved 50 yards

Gerd Niemann entered the Treptow NCO School near Rega on 1 April 1942. He left it eleven months later to join the armoured units. On 1 April 1943, he was made an NCO and transferred to the Panzer-Lehrkompanie 500 at Paderborn. For two months he followed a training course for Tiger crews, then on 26 May, he was assigned to 3 s. Pz. Abt. 503. At the end of the war he was kept prisoner for only twelve days. He rejoined the Bundeswehr where he remained until 1977, ending his career as Captain.
(Photo G. Niemann. Coll. D.L.)

when our tank was hit. All five of us got out unscathed. Hauptmann Mau, Leutnant Alt and Schmidt, the radio-operator sheltered under the tank. The driver, Fritz Meusel and myself, we hid behind the tracks.

"But a second shell then a third bent

Below: **This photograph shows clearly the sort of terrain on which Leutnant Weinert's crew found itself: a multitude of haystacks which concealed the enemy anti-tank guns. Once the tanks had been destroyed by these heavy guns, the Russian infantry left the edges of the woods and pounced on the crews when they were lucky enough to get out of their tank alive. The right wing of a Tiger can be identified in the foreground.** (© ECPAD DAT 3016 L15)

Hauptman Andreas Thaler, Kdr. of the II./Pz. Rgt. 25 was wounded by shrapnel during the first hours of the offensive; he was immediately replaced by Hauptmann Maul, CO of 6. Kp. who in turn was wounded, just after being appointed to his new command. (Photo J. Charita.)

Right: *Hauptmann Thaler was awarded the Knight's Cross on 13 January 1944 by Generalmajor Schulz, now the Kdr of the 7. Pz. Div. killed two weeks later.* (Photo J. Charita. Coll. D.L.)

the glacis of the tank upwards then exploded under the tank. Leutnant Alt was killed outright. Radio-Operator Schmidt lost an arm and Hauptmann Maul found himself on the ground after receiving a blow to the head.

"Frightened stiff, the driver and myself glanced at the fighting going on. I signalled Gefreiter Schmidt to come back with me to find the Kdr. of the regiment, Oberstleutnant Schulz, who was in a valley. A short time later, I reported what I had seen. I took two men to go and get Hauptmann Maul who was still lying next to the tank. I tried to reach him three times but enemy fire prevented me from doing so. Finally I managed to bring back Hauptmann Maul who was seriously wounded.

"For me there was no rest. With my documents in my map-case, I found myself radio-operator and I was often in the Abteilung's new commanding officer's tank. He got me to change codes everyday.

"Changing tanks didn't bring us any more luck. Only half an hour after we got settled in, the tank was hit by a shell and we had to find ourselves another machine.

"That evening the fighting stopped and we sheltered our tank in a dip in the ground. I got out to stretch a bit. Suddenly there was a terrible crackling sound then a blast of air which knocked me over. A mortar shell had just landed near me. At first I could feel no pain, then I realised that both my legs were bleeding profusely. I had been wounded by several splinters. So I was transported to the field hospital where I came across Hauptmann Mau who thanked me. As there were a lot of wounded crowded in the hospital, the surgeons were completely overwhelmed and could not operate everybody. This was why Hauptmann Maul died of his wounds several days later".

Von Rosen, the veteran, reports on the progress made by the 7.Pz. Div. and the 3./s. Pz. Abt. 503: "With the help of my four Tigers, Pz. Gren. Rgt.7 was able to enlarge the bridgehead and advance 13 km. The terrain was more or less open on the left but on the right, there was an abrupt elevation leading to a plateau on which was situated the village of Krutozh Log. The altitude varied by about 50 metres. This plateau, or vast plain, was 7. Pz. Div.'s objective.

"In the evening the scouts from Pz. AA 7 discovered a lane which was suitable for tanks enabling them to form a bridgehead on the heights".

In the evening of 5 July, the armoured corps'HQ drew up the following report concerning 7.Pz. Div.: "During the day, 7.Pz. Div. broke the first two enemy lines of defence. It has gathered on the heights situated to the east of Krutozh Log. It will therefore be able to head north-east in the next few hours."

7.Pz. Div.'s losses were light on the first day of the offensive: 10 killed and 86 wounded, a loss of 96 soldiers.

Leutnant von Rosen's Tiger 321. He was in command of 2./s. Pz.Abt. 503.

THE 19. PZ. DIV. SECTOR

The sector assigned to 19. Pz. Div. was located between 6. Pz. Div. and 7.Pz. Div. Its forces were spread out to the east of the village of Dalnizhe Peski which ran along the west bank of the Donets. The demarcation line with 7. Pz. Div. was the following: Repnoie (incl.) – Kolonozh-Dubovzh (not included) – Uroshaya Kolkoz (incl.), the river Rasumnaya from Kalinina to its source. The line with the 6. Pz. Div. passed by the Olschovez - Grasnozh road (incl.) – Supronovka – the fork crossroads to the north of Puschkamoie – northeast of Melikhovo – west of Werchene Olschanez.

The objective assigned to Generalleunant Schmidt consisted of getting hold of the heights overlooking Blishnaya Yigumenka using three Kampfgruppe.

During the night, sappers from Pz. Pi. Btl.19 worked non-stop to finish the wooden bridge, ready for the attack. Fortunately they were well trained for this type of work and handed over the bridge to the troops of Generalleutnant Schmidt, Kdr. of the division, on time. But there was another task waiting for the sappers: the east bank of the Donets had to be cleared of mines so that the leading units could move up in order to be able to attack. For the time being, there was no sign of life from the Russians who were supposed to be on the heights.

Using their detectors, the sappers started searching for mines. Their machines remained silent. Then they understood that the Russians had buried mines made

Hauptmann Gerhard Nemnich, Kdr of the Pz. Pi. Abt.19, receiving the Knight's Cross on 15 July in recognition of the bravery his sappers showed when opening up the way for the Pz. Rgt. 27 Panzers. He was killed on 15 March 1944 at Zepelin/Güstrow. (Photo J. Charita. Coll. D.L.)

of wood, undetectable with the apparatus they had.

It was a nightmare: they had to locate the mines using bayonets, and then defuse them as usual. This drawback delayed 9. Pz. Div.'s planned attack.

Suddenly a terrible barrage from the Russian artillery started, just a few minutes before the assault troops set out.

It struck Generalleutnant Schmidt then that the Russians knew perfectly well when the offensive was intended to start and most certainly what the strength of the troops engaged would be. Worse was still to come… The Stukas flying over the front line of his division reassured him a little. He saw them fall upon the Russian positions, unloading dozens of bombs in less than a minute.

Meanwhile, lying on the river bank, protected by the crossfire from Panzergrenadiere machine guns, the Pioniere cut through the tangles of barbed wire with their 24-in long wire-cutters. The sector was nothing but explosions, shouts, screams and howling engines. This was the beginning of Operation Citadel.

Oberst Goernemann's batteries from Pz. Art. Reg. 19 waited in vain for news from the artillery observers hidden on the heights. That is, their unsatisfactory view of the landscape prevented them from sending the vital information needed for covering the assault troops.

So it was without or almost without, artillery support that the Panzergrenadiere from Pz. Gren. Rgt.73 under Oberst Köhler started to attack. They had only one company of tank busters from the division battalion (Pz. Jg. Abt. 19) and elements of Pz. Pi. Btl.19. This was Kampfgruppe 73, one of the three assault groups of the 19. Pz. Div. It had a determining role to play because it was the vanguard of the other two Kampfgruppen in 19. Pz. Div., who had to wait for it to break through the Russian defences before reaching Uroshazah, near Kreida.

The second Kampfgruppe, placed on the left wing of the division, attacked the

Tiger 231 of 2./s. Pz.Abt. 503. The company lost 13 out of its 14 tanks on the first day of the offensive. They were very quickly repaired and were able to return to the fight.

Above:
Followed by Tigers 211 and 241, Tiger 231 is about to move down a secondary road to link up with some Landsers waiting for them in a village to carry out an attack. The tanks from 2./s. Pz. Abt. 503 lost 13 out of 14 tanks during the first day of the attack. They were repaired however after two or three days.
(© ECPAD DAT 3006 L5)

south of the Mikhailovka bridgehead.

It successfully reached the Razumnoe – Mikhailovka road but was ordered not to cross it. It had to wait for Köhler's forces before continuing its advance in the direction of Kreida. This Kampfgruppe was commanded by Oberleutnant Richter, the Kdr. of the Pz. Gren. Rgt. 74. He only disposed of his I. Btl. (the second being attached to Kgp Becker), 2./s. Pz. Abt. 503 and 3./Pz. Pi. Btl. 19.

From his position, Oberst Decker - Kdr. of the Pz. Abt.27 and the third Kampfgruppe (named after him) - anxiously watched the short flashes of light caused by explosions lighting up the network of Russian trenches.

He was waiting for the signal to attack to be given but this was delayed. His 81 crews waited for 2./s. Pz. Abt. 503 under Hauptmann Heilmann to open the way for them.

Why were the Tigers left lined up, parked and hidden along the river? Something important must have happened. Indeed the minefields precluded any advance. The Panzergrenadiere – I./Pz. Gren. Rgt. 74 – were stopped dead in their tracks and soon came under fire from the Russians who overlooked the area.

For the Belgorod sector alone - or simply to protect the Russian 81st Division's line of defence - the sappers from the 7th Russian Army had laid 2 133 anti-

tank mines and 2 626 anti-personnel mines every kilometre!

Moreover the Russian artillery demonstrated its efficiency thanks to its observers hidden in the highest place at Kreida station, a sort of water tower which Pz. Art. Rgt.19 gunners tried to take out during the day. They fired 22 000 shots at the Russians.

In the other artillery units, shells were being used up at an alarming rate. A report made at 16.15 stated that they would run out of ammunition by the end of the day. They would therefore have to be re-supplied if they were to back up the infantry when it attacked, and also bombard the enemy. Note that the ammunition supply was determined by the consumption of the previous day which was noted in a report. Authorised motorised transport capacity for the 19. Pz. Div. was 630 tonnes. Ten tonnes were supplied by horse; this may seem surprising for an armoured division.

Nevertheless, at around 7 o'clock, all this covering fire did not prevent the enemy from destroying the bridge built by the engineers and thereby preventing both Tigers and Sturmgeschütze from getting across to the east bank of the Donets.

Only towards 10 a.m. were Hauptmann Heilmann's 14 Tigers given the signal to start. On their way, the crews met dis-

traught and despairing Panzergrenadiere from II./Pz. Gren. Rgt. 74 returning from the front.

An observer from Pz. Art. Reg. 19 remembers the first few minutes when 2./s. Pz. Abt. 503's 14 Tigers were engaged. "The first Tiger was caught in the fire from a Russian machine gun which tried to stop it advancing. Quite unmindful of the bullets, the tank carried on. Another machine gun liberally sprayed the second Tiger, with just as much success. The Red Army soldiers thought they could set the two tanks on fire.

"It was then that the Russian bombers and fighters appeared trying to break up these charging Panzers accompanied by Panzergrenadiere. They dropped their bombs, strafed around a bit and then disappeared for the rest of the day."

The Tigers maintained their advance then they were stopped again to the east of hill 139.9. Tiger 224's loader and former Gefreiter Polzin remembers: *"After we got started, the whole company ran into a minefield. There was a violent blast*

backwards lifting our tank like straw. An enormous cloud of dust darkened the sector. The right track of our tank and the bogie wheels were damaged and the turret jammed. We discovered later that the front right also had been damaged and the clutch was out of order. When the reserve tank drove up to pick us up, our layer, Obergefreiter Liebermann, took the towing hawser over to hook on to the other tank. Unfortunately he was wounded doing this. Others followed: Gefreiter Eckart, Unteroffizier Naustedt and Unteroffizier Rudermann. This minefield cost our company 17 wounded.

"Profiting from our being towed towards the village, some infantrymen asked us to take back the body of their CO (Hauptmann) whom they were carrying in a piece of tent canvas. We placed him in between the driver and the radio operator, and then we reached the spot where the Tiger was going to be repaired. While we were repairing our tracks, Russian deserters who had surrendered in large numbers during the offensive were pushing the already rotting dead horses into ditches.

"Then Stalin's organs started greeting us, sending shrapnel all over the place. The Hauptmann's body, covered with dust, with only one arm and no legs was stretched out on the ground. His Iron Cross was still pinned to his smock. We struggled with our human feelings. We had to concentrate on the fact that we were going to be towed shortly to the repair workshop."

The other Tigers in 2. Kp. were ordered to come back. In order to protect them, batteries from Pz. Art. Rgt. 19 covered them by firing smoke grenades over the Russian positions. Only two Tigers were still operational.

A few days later, the Kdr. of s. Pz. Abt. 503, Hauptmann von Kageneck, wrote the following report to Gen. d. Pz. Tr. Breith: *"During the morning of 5 July 1943, we lost 13 Tigers out of the 14 engaged for a single company (2. Kp.)*

Nine were lost through mines and two or three days will be needed to get them repaired.

"The three causes of losses because of mines were the following:

1. From the very beginning, no map showed where German mines laid when the bridgehead was being established were located. There were two maps that could be consulted but they contradicted each other and both were inaccurate. Moreover two of our Tigers were directed towards our own mines that had just been primed. Then two other Tigers hit mines when crossing terrain that was thought to be safe.

2. The mines were cleared negligently. Three other Tigers were damaged by mines event though they had been assured that there weren't any where they were going.

(During the morning, two cannon from Pz. Art. Reg.74 also ran over mines although the road they were on was also supposed to have been cleared).

3. The eighth Tiger headed straight for an enemy minefield because the sappers told them it was quite safe to go ahead. The ninth Tiger also ran over a minefield when it wanted to change positions when Russian tanks attacked."

According to the original plan, the Tigers were to advance maintaining direct contact with the Panzergrenadiere, right behind the Engineer sections. The Tigers were however withdrawn from the front, leaving the Panzergrenadiere and the sappers to face the danger alone. In the evening of 5 July, four Tigers were 60-90 yards from the front held by infantry units.

Eight Tigers were missing for two or three days because of carelessness or

because they were badly used tactically which meant that they were not available to fulfil their role fighting enemy tanks and heavy guns.

On the evening of 5 July, ten Tigers from s. Pz. Abt. 503 were out of order. The following day, five of them had been repaired and had rejoined their respective companies. *"To these losses must be added four Panzers from Pz. Rgt. 27 which had been destroyed by direct hits,"* as reported by the KTB of 19 Pz. Rgt.

It was impossible to envisage taking Hill 139.9 for the time being. It was not only an observation post for the enemy but also an extraordinary position for the artillery which had taken Heilmann's Tigers and the Panzergrenadiere from I./Pz. Gren. Rgt. 74 to task.

The Kdr of 19. Pz. Div., Generalleutnant Schmidt, summarised the first day of the offensive as follows: *"The Russians fired so many cannon that I was convinced their artillery was more powerful than*

Generalleutnant Gustav Schmidt commanded the 19. Pz. Div. from 1 April 1942 to 7 August 1943 when he was killed near Borissovka. The remains of his division were retreating towards the southwest of Tomarovka when they were surprised by several Russian units.
Gustav Schmidt remained with 19. Pz. Div. during WWII. At the beginning of the conflict, as an Oberst, he commanded the Pz. Gren. Rgt. 74 and was awarded the Knight's Cross on 4 September 1940. He next commanded a brigade then was appointed Generalmajor in April 1942. He then received the German Gold Cross. On 1 January 1943 he was made Generalleutnant and was awarded the Oak Leaves on 6 March 1943. (Photo J. Charita. Coll. D.L.)

ours. The Russian mortars, hidden in the gorges, were silent when under fire from us. The 50-ton pontoons reserved for our Panzers were already out of action. Within ten minutes, the Russians overwhelmed our infantry with their hail of bullets. The division suffered heavy losses in men and materiel when crossing the Donets near Michailovka. The whole thing was almost a failure."

Meanwhile Gen.d.Pz. Tr. Breith drew up the following report for the Armee Abteilung Kempf: *"Of course, 19. Pz. Div. was held up on the right wing of the Donets which it tried to cross. Then its advance was slowed down by the many minefields."*

Compared to what was reported, the Köhler and Richter Panzergrenadiere Groups had actually gained quite a lot of terrain because they had destroyed the Russian's first line of defence. The first Kampfgruppe was established at Kreida station, situated less than a kilometre from the town and Oberleutnant Richter's tactical group was situated near hill 139.9 which it hoped to capture the following day with the help of its only SPW company. Once these heights were eliminated, Oberst Becker could finally intervene with his Tiger regiment which for the time being was assembled at the rear. Losses for the day stood at 62 killed, 413 wounded and 22 missing, a total of 497 soldiers

Below:
Smiling Landsers file past the reporter. The third soldier from the left is carrying a Panzerfaust on his shoulder. Because it was hot these men have hooked their heavy helmet by the chinstrap onto the left hand clasp of their heavy belts. Some are wearing forage caps according to the regulations, other are not. "During WWII German soldiers were very relaxed where the wearing of uniforms was concerned. This is no longer the case in the Bundeswehr." says Generalmajor von Rosen.
(© ECPAD DAT 3006 L38)

A British Valentine Mk I tank destroyed at Kursk. The Valentine was in service in the Red Army from the end of 1941. It was used mainly in the south of Russia because of its resistance to heat. Although thick armour enabled it to withstand enemy fire, insufficient speed and inadequate firepower from its 40-mm canon meant it was only a second-rate tank. Later it was fitted out with a 75-mm canon. Based on the A10 Cruiser tank, the Valentine first saw the light of day in England in 1938. With all its different variants, the Valentine was produced in greater numbers – almost 7 000 - than any other tank for the British Army during WWII. (BA 22/630/7a)

THE SECOND DAY OF THE OFFENSIVE: 6 JULY 1943

Gen. d. Pz. Tr. Breith's headquarters drew up a bold but complex plan. Its objective was to prevent the enemy intervening from the east by sending units in this direction.

Heeresgruppe South HQ feared however that this manoeuvre would dangerously thin out the east flank of II/SS-Pz. Korps. Gen. d. Pz. Tr. Breith's plan had the 19. Pz. Div. protecting them by covering the Belgorod and Mikhailovka bridgeheads, before heading for the Donets valley. The final objective was to reach the Denzh Yuroshaya Kolkoz.

THE 6. PZ. DIV. SECTOR

The advance units of the 6. Pz. Div. were relieved by the 168 I.D. which played an important part in Operation Citadel. StuG. Abt. 228's battery, reinforcing 6. Pz. Div., was attached to 168 I.D. Generalmajor von Hünersdorff division's retreated despite being harassed by the Russians. Pz. Rgt. 11's tactical armoured group assembled in the Kolonozh-Dubovzh sector, to the

rear of 7. Pz. Div. then headed to the west of Pz. Rgt. 25 under Oberstleutnant Schülz (7 Pz. Div.). The day's objective was to reach the south bank of the Rasumnaya in order to cross the bridges near Solomino. The group would then attack Generalovka and stop finally a kilometre to the south of Jastrebovo.

But the Panzergruppe set off only at lunchtime after wasting precious time assembling.

Accompanied by scouts and still ahead of his troops, Oberst von Oppeln Bronikowski came into sight of a bridge which his armoured group would have to cross protected by Panzergrenadiere. He met the officer holding the bridge who encouraged him to hurry up and cross over quickly since the bridge was soon likely fall into Russian hands.

An hour later all the armour was across and at 14.30, they reached the bridgehead set up by Pz. Rgt. 25 near

CO of 11./Pz. Rgt. 25, Oberleutnant Hans Ohrloff was awarded the Knight's Cross on 27 July 1941. After being held prisoner for a long time after the war, he took up a military career with the Bundeswehr in 1955. In April 1969 he was Kdr. of the Panzerbrigade 29, in October 1970, he was Generalmajor and Kdr. of the 3. Pz. Div., in October 1974 he commanded the I. Korps. (Photo J. Charita. Coll. D.L.)

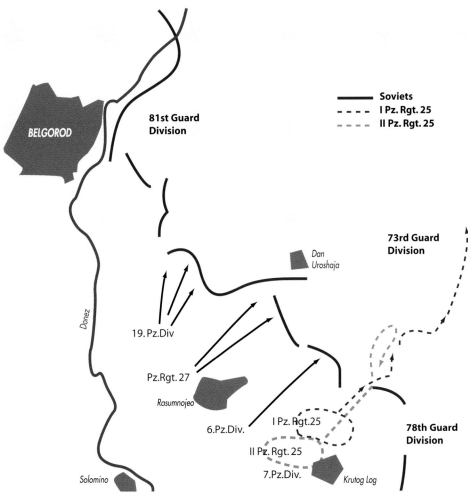

81st Guard Division

BELGOROD

73rd Guard Division

Dan Uroshaja

19. Pz.Div.

Pz.Rgt. 27

Rasumnojeo

6.Pz.Div.

I Pz. Rgt.25

II Pz. Rgt. 25

78th Guard Division

7.Pz.Div.

Krutog Log

Solomino

Donez

Legend:
— Soviets
– – – I Pz. Rgt. 25
– – – II Pz. Rgt. 25

SITUATION AT THE FRONT OF THE III. PZ. KORPS. ON 6 JULY 1943.
(AFTERT GENERALMAJOR VON ROSEN).

Below:
British Mathilda II tanks delivered under the Lend-Lease agreements were encountered during the battle of Kursk. Although slow and weakly-armed (one 40-mm canon), they were much appreciated by the crews for their thick armour. (DR Caption: M. Chaubiron.)

pated during the whole conflict.

The attack was organised in the following way: ten Tigers from 1./s. Pz. Abt. 503 were right at the front of the attack, closely followed by Pz. Rgt. 11's HQ.

The 5. and 7./Pz. Rgt. 11 followed on the right with 8. Kp. setting itself up on the left. The SPW of II./Pz. Gren. Rgt. 114 under Hauptmann Neckernauer were ready to intervene.

The Russians brought their artillery to bear on the battle and their fighters flew around in swarms until the Tigers started to stream over the Russian positions; the fighters then disappeared from the skies for fear of hitting their own men.

Franz Kurowski states that Oberst von Oppeln Bronikowski added some very interesting details concerning this tank charge:

"Our tanks went through two deeply entrenched Russian positions before reaching the River Penna. Then our cannon set off lightning and thunder like you only get during storms. Our firepower got the better of the Russian bunkers. Several very short salvoes destroyed the enemy anti-tank guns. Several of our tanks (Author's note: three) were stopped when they ran over some mines.

"Nevertheless the enemy's defensive front was shattered. It was 6. and 7 Pz. Rgt. 11 under Major Bäke supported by the tanks from 1./s. Pz. Abt.503 that made contact with Pz. Rgt. 25. Seven enemy tanks, ten anti-tank guns as well as a large number of enemy guns were destroyed. I learnt that Dr Bäke had

Razumnoe. After elements of Pz. Rgt. 6 came up in support, the attack on Generalovka started at 16.45. After the war, Oberst von Oppeln Bronikowski declared that this was the biggest engagement in which he had partici-

Left :

Major Franz Bäke commanded the II./Pz. Rgt. 11 during Operation Citadel. On the left, his Adjudant, Hauptmann Herbert from II./Pz. Rgt. 11's StabsKompanie. Note the coded insignia of 6. Pz. Div. painted on the command Panzer III's structure. Franz Bäke was 19 when he joined the artillery during WWI. After the war he studied to become a dentist. He joined the armoured troops in August 1939 and became company commander then very shortly afterwards CO of the II./Pz. Rgt. 11 in 1942. In November 1943, he took command of Pz. Rgt. 11 then the Panzer Brigade Feldherrnhalle in July 1944. Two months before the German capitulation, he was promoted to Generalmajor and given command of 13 Pz. Div. Because he was able to prove that he had always respected his military commitment and had had nothing to do with politics, he remained in prison for barely two years. He died in 1978 at Hagen.
(© ECPAD 1945 L06)

Left

The soldiers in the III. Pz. Korps took advantage of being in a kolkhoz to stock up. While Ukrainian civilians load sacks of wheat or any other cereal on the Panjewagen, Major Bäke, Kdr. of II./Pz. Rgt. 11 talks to a Leutnant, probably from the 6. Pz. Div. signals company.
(DAT 3029 L29)

Bottom :

One of the rare photographs showing a kolkhoz during the German occupation in the Ukraine. These collective farms appeared in 1929, a creation of the Soviet regime which rejected any notions of private enterprise. The peasants who lived near these collective units were paid according to the quality and the quantity of the cereal produced. When German troops occupied the Ukraine, they were tolerant with the population who opened up its schools again and started printing its own liberal papers. As for the peasants they rushed to the ever-so hated kolkhoz to destroy them. But those few months of happiness were soon quashed with the arrival of ReichsKommissar Erich Koch at the end of 1941. In total accord with Nazi doctrine, he rapidly set up the mass exploitation of Ukrainian resources. Treating the inhabitants like sub-humans, Koch had the schools closed and the Ukrainians colonised in the most awful way possible. He tolerated independent Ukrainian political activity only because it was an anti-communist. The presence of this kolkhoz at the rear of the III. Pz. Korps was a true godsend for the soldiers.
(DAT 3025 L24)

Right:
The drivers of these six beautifully lined-up Renault AHR trucks are talking quietly before going back their respective tasks. Indeed there are vehicles from two different arms here. The first truck bears the tactical sign of 7./Pz. Rgt. 11 above which can be seen the initials Op for Oppeln Bronikowski, then the insignia of 6. Pz. Div. half-hidden by the light. The frame painted on the vehicle door denotes the class of vehicle: category, total weight and weight category. The other trucks come from the Pz. Nachtr. Abt. 82 under Oberleutnant Moll. The type of camouflaged the units was totally different. The Renault AHRs were powered by a six-cylinder engine. They weighed five tonnes and had a top speed of 59 kph (39 mph). They were produced in great numbers between 1941 and 1944 to replace the different trucks which had been requisitioned by the Germans.
(DAT 3029 L16)

again destroyed another T-34."

When the tactical group came into sight of Generalovka, it was taken to task by the Russian artillery. As a result, the Panzergrenadiere battalion's SPW withdrew, leaving the terrain to the Tigers from 1./s. Pz. Abt. 503 accompanying the Panzers of 6. and 7. Kp.

In a combined assault, these three tank companies attacked the last remaining Russian positions around Generalovka. Once these were crushed under a deluge of shells, Kampfgruppe Glaesemer appeared with its SPW full of Panzergrenadiere. The bursting shells which hit the thin armour did not discourage these highly-trained soldiers from jumping to the ground to wipe out any remaining resistance.

While untold tragedies were taking place in the hell of what was Generalovka's main street, the Panzers from 6. And 7. Kp. hurried off to the Solovzhev Kolkhoz which they captured at the same time. As for the other Pz. IIIs and IVs from II./Pz. Rgt. 11, they fought the Russian 31st Anti-Tank Battalion for the Hills 216.1 and 207.9.

As far as the Tiger crews were concerned, they were appalled when they discovered they were in a minefield and under fire from anti-tank guns. Hauptmann Burmester called the Pioniere. Elements from the Pi. Btl. 70, a unit directly attached to III. Pz. Korps tried to get the Tigers out of this sticky situation. Several times, the sappers needed the Tigers' help clearing the mines. They proceeded as follows:

Right:
Three young section commanders from the armoured Abteilung of Pz. Rgt. 11 listening to a Sonderführer who has bought himself a locally made cap. He has two campaign ribbons over his right pocket. His rank entitled him too wear officer's breeches and to have a map-case. Had he been in the infantry, he would have been a Leutnant. In the background, the tactical sign of 6. Pz. Div. can be seen on the front of the vehicles.
(DAT 3029 L15)

day, Reutermann made contact with Pz. Rgt. 25 which 3./s. Pz. Abt. 503 was fighting with.

The crews of 1./ s. Pz. Abt. 503 and Pz. Rgt. 11 destroyed seven tanks (six T-34s and one T 70), 10 anti-tank guns, one canon, three 17.2 cm cannon, four 7.62-cm anti-aircraft guns and killed 120 enemy soldiers during the day.

Panzergruppe von Oppeln Bronikowski lost eight tanks including Pz 905 belonging to Leutnant Knut (StabsKompanie) who continued fighting aboard another tank. Mines destroyed three others.

At nightfall, II./Pz. Rgt. 11 took every precaution when set it self up defensively near Hill 209.9. They were right to be cautious because the Russians attacked but were driven off without difficulty. Kampfgruppe Unrein, attached to Abteilung Bäke set up its position around Belinskaya.

6. Pz. Div. headed for the Generalovka area to support 19. Pz. Div. during its attack on Blishnaya Yigumenka. The anti-aircraft guns of I./ Flak Abt. 138 were being moved up for air defence. The Panzergrenadiere of the II Battalion were in front of Kolonozh-Dubovzh, making a protective screen for the division which was assembling.

attaching six or seven yard-long poles to the Tigers, they suspended rollers made of wood from them and then, when one of the rollers hit a mine it exploded.

But this time, while clearing this minefield, the sappers suffered such heavy casualties that the attack had to be suspended. Hauptmann Burmester's Tigers continued the mission later.

Panzergruppe von Oppeln Bronikowski's situation was scarcely more enviable: its 6. and 7./Pz. Rgt. 11 had been terribly weakened especially Oberstleutnant Reutermann's unit. The stubborn Russian resistance did finally yield however in the face of the fury shown by the armoured group. At the end of the

Below: *The KV1s, which were even more heavily armoured than the T-34s, could do nothing against the more powerful Tigers.* (DR)

THE 7. PZ. DIV. SECTOR

At 5 o'clock, Generalmajor von Funck's division started off from the heights situated to the north of Krutozh-Log to attack those near Hill 216.1, to the west of Batrazkaya Datscha Kolkhoz.

Covered by Leutnant von Rosen's Tiger section which had set itself up during the night on a high plateau, the Panzers of I./Pz. Rgt. 25 attacked towards the northeast.

Ex-Leutnant von Rosen recalls: *"I had two speakers in my tank. The first was tuned to Oberstleutnant Schülz's HQ's frequency and the second to 3./s. Pz. Abt. 503's. Since Pz. Rgt. 25 did not have any ammunition for my four Tigers, I go some through 3.Kp. My mission was to break through the supposed line of defence with a front-line company from 7. Pz. Div., then to attack (or not) in the direction of Batrazkaya Datscha. At any rate we had to go far into enemy territory.*

Getting on to the high plateau was difficult, but there were no incidents. On the way, I noticed a wooded plateau on my right. It worried me. We got closer carefully then I waited till the armoured Abteilung came up.

"I opened up my turret to find a Red Army soldier near me in a foxhole. He looked at me angrily. I made a sign to him to surrender behind the tank but he refused to obey. I took my pistol and made him understand what he'd get if he didn't obey. No reaction. I fired a shot near him on purpose, several times. No reaction. Then I took a grenade, pulled out the pin and threw it in his direction. The Russian picked it up and threw it back at my tank. Faced with such stubbornness, I gave up. He was taken prisoner by the Panzergrenadiere following us.

"Finally I./Pz. Rgt. 25 reached its positions on the heights after a particularly hard climb. We approached the forest which turned out to be impenetrable. On my right, I saw a clearing which we headed for; but it was so narrow that we couldn't get through. I glanced to the right: there were no anti-tank guns. I looked all about me."

"Suddenly on the left edge of the forest, five or six flashes of lightning shot out. T-34s! We took some of them out and so, after trying us they pulled back a bit. We headed for a quiet spot. That was the end of the encounter. Thank God no shells hit the bogey wheels. I

Above:*The formidable ISU 152 or SU 152 self-propelled gun with its 152-mm canon. This heavy self-propelled gun was built for the Red Army at the Battle of Stalingrad. It was the only thing capable of destroying a Tiger at long distance during the summer of 1943.* (DR)

can't remember how many we destroyed.

"It was now risky crossing the clearing. Apparently the Russians hadn't set up anything nearby or else, they just let us go through on purpose. We later learnt that those anti-tank guns were there since they had fired at Pz. Rgt.

25's light armour.

"We continued clearing up the terrain. Pz. Rgt. 25's Tigers following us were reassuring. Thanks to the map I noticed that we were in front of a hill which would put us off course from our planned line of attack.

"Through a clearing in front of me I

Below: **On 6 July 1943, six of these ISU 152s or SU 152s were destroyed by s. Pz. Abt. 503 in the Krutozh Log sector.** *Leutnant von Rosen recalls: "Suddenly I spotted SU 152 self-propelled assault guns which we hadn't noticed. They were well camouflaged but very slow to fire. My two Tigers placed on my right immediately opened fire, well before the Russians. On the first explosion, one of the guns blew up in a cloud of very thick black smoke."* (DR)

could see another hill about a half mile and a half, way behind the Russian lines of defence. Suddenly twenty shells fell in front of us. Innumerable anti-tank guns dug in in front of the hill had just opened fire. We about-turned and got under cover. If it had been a strong concentration of armour we would not have had a chance of surviving. I radioed 'Stopped. Air Force needed.' A short while later, I got a reply: 'Luftwaffe coming in 30 minutes.'

"On this summer's day, inside our tank, the heat was unbearable. We were thirsty and drenched in sweat. Our faces and hands were blackened by powder. We could get a bit of cooler air by leaving the turret hatch open (...)

"Then there was a fantastic sight: wave after wave of Stukas fell upon the Russian positions with their sirens screaming: all hell was let loose; the last machines had barely disappeared before we were ordered to get going again. We moved forward without hindrance. We then went through a narrow passage between a forest and a hill from which we discovered the enemy positions totally destroyed. It had been a hard nut to crack but we'd done it.

"I headed our Panzer towards the edge of a forest. My four other Tigers were on my right. Suddenly there was a powerful bang: the tank made like a series of little jumps. Unteroffizier Ziegler, our driver, stopped the tank immediately. I opened the hatch and saw that part of the right hand track had unrolled behind us. We had passed over a mine.

"With the on-board radio, I informed my section and the regiment. First we were told to stop then that the furthermost company would carry on our reconnaissance mission instead. Two Tigers from my section reinforced this company. The third, Oberfeldwebel Burgis', tank stayed close to ours to cover us. My layer and I made sure that the track was not lying on another mine. The damage turned out to be superficial. The tank was still on its damaged track but this had unrolled completely.

"We started by making sure that there weren't any more mines around us. The radio operator remained inside the tank, near the radio. We found a dozen or so wooden mines on the edge of the forest: we got rid of them very quickly. They were only covered in grass. We removed the detonators without any danger. All tank commanders had been trained in mine clearing before Operation Citadel.

"The Regiment's Panzers were moving up in front of us. The Kdr., Oberstleutnant Schülz, drew up alongside me – All was well. I would follow the column when my tank was ready.

"We then noticed that we had to unroll the tracks again because three links had to be changed. That was enough to break your back. To my great relief I saw a small group of supply trucks belonging to the armoured regiment coming up. A one-ton Zugsmaschine from our 3. Kp.'s ordnance group was with them. These half-tracks always followed the tanks in case one of them broke down.

The mechanics got down to work with skill and we were soon ready to go again. The damage done to the runner wheels wasn't important and could be repaired later.

"We followed the regiment's tracks that led us towards Badratskaya Datscha. The leading units had come across another heavily fortified line of defence, except for the right flank which was still unprotected.

"We positioned ourselves hedgehog-fashion and for the rest of the day we remained in the area. We were re-supplied during the night. We were able to fill up with fuel, ammunition, oil for the engines and coolant. 'First the horse, then the rider,' was the traditional order, straight from the cavalry regulation manual. It was still in use with the armoured arm: the tank was re-supplied first; it was got ready for combat. Only then could the crew look after itself. We went to sleep behind our tank, not for long but just like logs."

Leading the attack against the 73rd Infantry Division of the Guard and followed by Pz. IIIs and IVs from II./Pz.Rgt. 25, the 3. Kp. (except for the 2nd Section) Tigers under Oberleutnant Scherf, opened the way for the other 7. Pz.Div. units. They got into Razumnoe and Krutozh Log. Serious difficulties faced Oberstleutnant Schülz, trying to lead his armoured regiment through all these woods and valleys where the Russians were hiding, waiting for them with their anti-tank guns and bazookas.

Just before dawn, Oberst Glaesener's

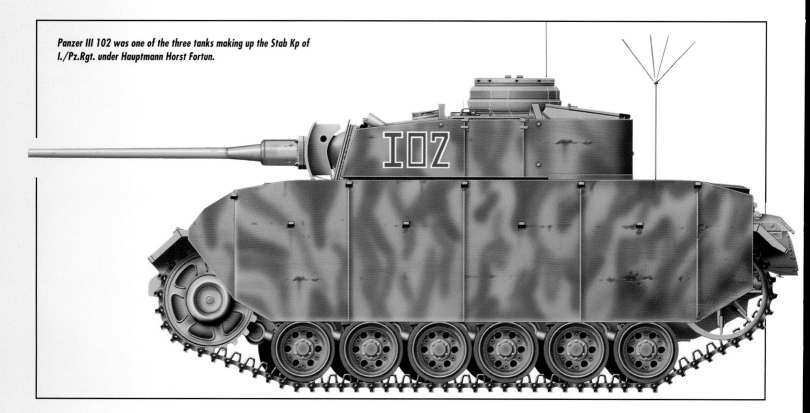

Panzer III 102 was one of the three tanks making up the Stab Kp of I./Pz.Rgt. under Hauptmann Horst Fortun.

Kampfgruppe - Pz.Gren.Rgt.6 – attacked to the north of Krutozh Log with the intention of reaching Hill 216.1. But the Germans, shaken by the fire from heavy weapons, had to break off and wait for day-break. They had fallen into a real trap. Oberst Glaesener decided to form two assault groups supported by the half-section of mortars and heavy machine guns.

Meanwhile the Russians had got so close to the Panzergrenadiere positions that they could be heard whispering. Oberst Glaesener and his men noticed that the enemy seemed to be very agitated and they wanted to know how many of them there were.

The COs of the two assault groups gave orders to attack separately, one after the other. The soldiers followed each other opening fire on where they supposed the enemy positions were. Some Russian infantrymen got out as fast as they could, bullets whistling around their ears. Others were mown down in their shelters by a few short MP40 bursts. The Panzergrenadiere gradually pushed the Russians back inside the forest. But snipers hiding in the trees started aiming at the officers, some of whom fell with a bullet straight through the head. Resistance from the Russians was stiffening, and stiffening very quickly, their firepower reaching an intensity which hitherto had very rarely been encountered on the Eastern Front by even these war-hardened Panzergrenadiere.

Oberst Glaesener now knew he would not be able to reach the heights for several hours now and that Panzergruppe Schülz would have to do without him.

In a letter to his wounded ordnance officer, Oberstleutnant Schülz recounted what happened on this, the second day: "The armoured spearhead was blocked in front of a wood. Even the Tigers couldn't get near. Two of them were hit. The anti-tank guns on the left and the artillery on the right started shooting.

"We advanced cautiously attacking from the right, but we were halted. We could do nothing in spite of support from Schmückle's artillery group. I was forced to let Weitzel's battalion lead the attack on foot without my being able to support him.

"Hauptmann Fortun drew up a plan and launched the tanks from his Abteilung on the left. Our artillery fired a few shots ahead of his unit but the observers could not see well enough to guide the gunners properly."

Hauptmann Horst Fortun, Kdr of I./Pz.Rgt. 25. He was born on 4 March 1917 at Neustadt in East Prussia. He was awarded the Knight's Cross posthumously on 7 July 1943. He had won the Iron Cross, Second Class on 6 October 1939 and the Iron Cross, First Class on 29 July 1940 then the German Gold Cross on 2 April 1942 while he was in command of 2./Pz.Rgt. 25.
(Photo J. Charita. Coll. D.L.)

Hermann Rothe, a veteran who took part in this attack, recalls: "The order was given by the Kdr. of I./Pz.Rgt. 25. It was 'Mit Vollgas heran.' (Go flat out). My old battalion set off with determination under Hauptmann Fortun, without firing a single shot... And it worked! Soon we found ourselves at the edge of a forest. Several of our tanks carried on. Six unfortunately received direct hits and three of them were already on fire. But we succeeded.

"Unfortunately Hauptmann Fortun was seriously wounded in his tank. He was taken straight away to a first aid post but he died on the way. He was an extraordinary man. Little Lauersen who was always so happy was also killed. To which must be added the loss of a crew from 2. Kp. and other Panzerschützen."

Generalmajor von Funcke's 7. Pz.Div. fought all day without letting up in order to reach the Krutozh Log heights where the Russian regiment had set itself up just like in a fortress. It was so well entrenched that there was a risk of it wiping out most of the 106. I.D. from XI. A.K. But in the end, it was the Russian regiment which got caught in the trap, well before the German infantry division needed to worry.

At the beginning of the morning 106 I.D. suffered heavy losses from Russian aircraft; it then ventured too far forward into the marshes which delayed its advance to Krutozh Log.

In order to support 7. Pz.Div.'s right flank, 106 I.D. and the other divisions in XI A.K. now had to put up a dogged resistance. Surprisingly, in less than two days, these infantry divisions had advanced more than ten kilometres (6 _ miles) into 7th Guards Army territory, which was a real performance for these divisions given their limited means of transport.

An Ilyushin B2, better known as the Shturmovik (attacker). This famous ground attack plane was heavily armoured and renowned for its endurance and its capacity for punishment.
(DR - Caption by M. Chaubiron)

Next page top left: *The AA gun commander scrutinises the sky with his 10 x 50 binoculars. He is wearing an Iron Cross, First Class on the smock of his Luftwaffe combat dress.* (BA 22/2926/32)

Next page top right: *The gun is skilfully set up and two of its four barrels start spitting fire at a hellishly infernal rate. Strangely enough, one of the servers seems to be removing one of the barrels.* (BA 22/2926/38)

Next page bottom left: *Flieger Alarm!" The enemy plane has been spotted and the servers are at their posts. Once the platform sides were lowered, the soldiers could shoot at the plane whilst turning the gun right through 360°.* (BA 22/2926/37)

Next page bottom right: *This shot enables us to see another Flak Vierling server. The Luftwaffe ground combat insignia is clearly visible on his four-pocketed jacket.* (BA 22/2926/33)

Above:
Flak servers have put up a tent near their 2-cm Flakvierling 38 auf Fahrgetsell Zugkraftwagen 8t. The total crew manning this machine numbered at least 10.
(BA 22/2926/27)

Once 106 I.D. was up to attacking Krutozh Log and the situation was clearer, II./Pz.Rgt. 25 and 3./s. Pz.Abt. 503 (less the 2nd section) followed in the tracks of I./Pz.Rgt. 25. These units ran into heavy fire coming from the edge of a forest situated within the Russian second line of defence. A few hours later, they managed to get on the right flank of I./Pz.Rgt. 25. Once the two

Abteilungen had united, they attacked the little town of Rasumnoe; there was a large concentration of Russian armour in the vicinity.

Oberstleutnant Schülz had an unbelievable stroke of luck because the CO of the Russian tanks was in no way an experienced or cool-headed officer and the results were terrible. Schülz's tank-men wiped out the armoured unit. No fewer than thirty-four T-34 wrecks were strewn all over the battlefield at sundown.

"After this engagement, Oberleutnant Scherf's Tigers (3. Kp.) took on the cap-

ture of the Badratskaya Datscha Kolkhoz where the defensive fire was heavier than the previous day," recalls the veteran Gerd Niemann, from Tiger 311, *"but my Tiger was incapable of following up on the attack because of the number of direct hits it had taken. Leutnant Weinert (his Panzerkommandant) exchanged it for Tiger 313."*

The outcome of the engagement was very uncertain for the rest of Generalmajor von Funck's division. Opposing them were well-camouflaged, seasoned Russian troops, well dug in on the edge of a forest on a hill. The historian, Paul Carell, says: *"There, the division was pinned down by raking artillery fire and the Pz.Rgt. 25 tanks were not able to come to their rescue."*

Nevertheless it has to be remembered that Pz.Rgt. 25 had not only captured Batrazkaya Datscha but broken the enemy's second line of defence a mile to the north of Hill 209.6. This success enabled 106 I.D. to carry out a successful attack on the right, allowing Schülz to take Hill 216.1 directly and on these heights, he was able to make contact with 106 I.D.

7. Pz.Div's. front line stretched from the woods situated a mile and a quarter to the northeast of Krutozh Log – Hill 164.7 – Generalovka. The fighting carried on in Pz.Rgt. 25's zone to the southwest of Hill 216.1.

For the day's fighting, there were 133 casualties, including 28 killed in 7. Pz.Div. On this subject, Hermann Rothe

Left:
First light: one of the soldiers brings water bottles and billies to his comrades.
(BA 22/2926/28)

Left:
After leaving Pz.Rgt. 25 HQ and the s. Pz.Abt. 503 repair workshop, the P.K. carries on his report by crossing the zone assigned to the 168 I.D. which was situated to the west of the Donets. Horse-drawn units played an important role backing up the armoured elements of the III. Pz.Korp.
(BA 22/2923/16a)

from I./Pz.Rgt. 25 wrote: *"We lost Feldwebel Pfaller and Unteroffizier Rauen from Armoured Regiment HQ, as well as Funckmeister Blaschke who was wounded. Thalen and the dispatch rider Schupke were also killed…"*

As for 3./s. Pz.Abt. 503, it lost two dead at Krutozh Log and three at Batrazkaya Datscha. The servers of I./Flak Rgt. 61, who had been attached to Generalmajor von Funck's armoured division for the day, distinguished themselves in particular.

THE 19. PZ.DIV. SECTOR

During the night of 5 to 6 July, Generalleutnant Schmidt's armoured division moved through the wooded area situated to the southeast of Mikhailovka, then headed south-westwards before pivoting northwards, from Dan Yurozhaya.

But for 19. Pz.Div. the attack got bogged down again. Pz.Rgt. 27's tanks finally reached the Razumnoe-

Mikhailovka road, which Köhler's and Richter's Panzergrenadiere had crossed the previous day, but were obliged to halt because the ground was thick with mines. It was 3.30.

Oberst Becker, the Kdr. of this armoured regiment, was furious. The day was going to be just as disastrous as the previous one. He had just lost 18 tanks without his armoured regiment even being engaged. He decided to stop the attack and refer immediately to Generalleutnant Schmidt who then explained the situation to his staff. Schmidt and his officers decided to change the original plan and concentrate their efforts on Razumnoe-North. So that they would get the most

Below:
The reporter meets a large HQ where there are officers from the armoured arm and the army. Coordination between the two arms was indispensable. Both the Panzer officer and the Heer officer are wearing the German Cross on their smocks.
(BA 22/2923/19a)

Above:
Generalmajor von Hünersdorff studying the map with the Major seen above. He has put his rubberised trench coat back on; the weather was very variable during the Battle of Kursk.
(BA 22/2923/23)

Top right :
Generalmajor von Hünersdorff is sitting in the grass on the side of the track just like an ordinary soldier with his double-breasted jacket unbuttoned; he is sitting on his trench coat on which he has laid his belt and his holster.
(BA 22/2923/21a)

right:
Generalmajor von Hünersdorff settling into a light radio reconnaissance vehicle fitted with an MG 34 with an armoured shield. The crew comprises four men. They are aboard a light Sd Kfz 250/3 or radio vehicle. It weighed 5.35 tonnes. With its FUG 7 and its FUG 8, they could be in liaison with divisional headquarters and the air force.
(BA 22/2923/24a)

Left :
Tross' men bringing petrol for 6. Pz.Div.'s tanks. One of them is wearing the Heer's camouflage smock which had just been issued. (BA 22/2923/27u)

Below :
Hauptmann Necknauer, Kdr. of II./Pz.Gren.Rgt.114, has approached the half-track to listen to what von Hünersdorff has to say. Despite the difference in rank between these two officers, the Hauptmann has not put out his cigarette. Both their faces are gaunt from fatigue. (BA 22/2923/29a)

Next page left:
Generalmajor von Hünersdorff was born in Cairo on 28 November 1898. He took part in WWI as an officer, remaining in the Reichswehr after the conflict. When the next war broke out, he held the rank of Major and left the 253. I.D. to become Chief-of Staff of the II. Armeekorps, then of Panzergruppe 3 from February 1941. After Operation Barbarossa he was promoted to Oberst and awarded the German Gold Cross. On 22 December 1942, he was awarded the Knight's Cross. He was given command of Pz.Rgt.11 which remained under his command till his death. He tried to break the noose around Stalingrad with his tanks but did not succeed. On 1 May 1943, he was wearing a Generalmajor's epaulettes when he took over as Kdr. of the 6. Pz.Div. On 13 July in the morning he was slightly wounded in the head but in the afternoon he was wounded in the head again by shrapnel, this time seriously. He was awarded the Oak Leaves while he was in hospital and died three days later. (BA 22/2923/33a)

Next page right: *Generalmajor von Hünersdorff jumps to the ground while his Sd Kfz of the II./Pz.Gren.Rgt.114 manoeuvres a hundred yards or so from their Kdr.* (BA 22/2923/36a)

from their forces and succeed in this new mission, Gren. Rgt. 442 of 168 I.D. was attached for the time being to Kampfgruppe Becker.

At the beginning of the afternoon, the German artillery lengthened its range and Oberst Becker's Panzers attacked the Razumnoe sector with the support of the Landsers from 168 I.D. They progressed satisfactorily until they reached a kolkhoz where mines once more halted their advance.

Not content with having to wait for the way to be opened up for him, Oberst Becker skilfully launched the Panzergrenadiere from I./Pz.Gren.Rgt. 74 against the heights situated to the west of the kolkhoz. They suffered heavy losses when they ran into the Russians who had set up fortified positions.

This battalion was the backbone of the Becker Kampfgruppe. Richter's men had become specialists in infiltrating the Russian lines. From the top of the newly conquered hills they could now espy their next objective: Yuroshaya.

At about 16.00, a handful of soldiers who had volunteered to go out and reconnoitre, reached a wood which was only three hundred yards from the village. A short while later, they returned to report the extent of the Russian defences to Oberst Becker. Knowing then that Razumnoe could be taken by surprise, Becker decided to launch an attack with Panzergrenadiere from I./Pz.Gren.Rgt.74 supported by a few Panzers.

Before the Panzergrenadiere streamed over the Russian infantry positioned defensively in front of and inside the town, Oberstleutnant Goernemann let off a heavy barrage at the buildings. When they returned, the civilians found their town devastated. An hour later, the village was in Oberst Becker's hands.

This attack took place in the zone assigned to the Russian 81st Infantry Division and got the latter's command - who were not expecting any attack in this direction - to react. Alarming news started to reach headquarters: its troops positioned facing the Mikhailovka bridgehead and to the west of the Donets had been forced to withdraw. As a result, divisional units placed in reserve were ordered to reinforce the units which were already engaged. But it took them until 22.00 to get up into the line.

In the meantime Generalleutnant Schmidt was ordered to establish a stronghold to the west of Razumnoe.

For 19. Pz.Div., the fighting continued in the Blishnaya Yigumenka and Delnazhaya Yigumenka sectors, near Sabynino where the Russian 81st Infantry Division was almost wiped out. Oberst Becker's Panzers had their

168 I.D.

Kdr.:	Generalmajor Chales de Beaulieu
Gren. Rgt. 417:	Major Barkmann
Gren. Rgt. 429:	Major Vollmary
Gren. Rgt. 442:	Major Bingemer (?)
Art. Rgt. 248:	Oberst Proff
Aufkl.Abt. 248:	Rittmester Schlemminger (?)
Pz.Jg. Abt. 248:	Oberleutnant von Jordan
Pi.Btl. Btl. 248:	Oberleutnant Holz
Nachr. Abt. 248:	Oberleutnant Bitsch (?)
Div. Nachsch. Tr.:	(?)

revenge and the savage fighting for the capture of Kreida carried on. The Kdr. of Kampfgruppe 73, Oberst Köhler, went up the lines where he met one of his battalion commanders busy talking with a company commander. They were worried by the heavy losses suffered by their units and flabbergasted by the Russians' stubborn resistance.

When Oberst Köhler was told about his regiment's heavy losses, due mainly to artillery, the only thing he could do was report that his unit had suffered heavy casualties and that it had to be reinforced. The III. Pz.Korps Stab sent him I./Gren. Rgt. 429. These Grenadiere made the long journey through unsafe forests and reached them in the middle of the afternoon.

"We are now under artillery fire. The Russkis have positioned their guns about 1 500 yards away and they are preventing us from entering this town", the Oberleutnant announced to Oberst Köhler.

At about midday, to the Panzergrenadiere's great surprise, the Russians counter-attacked from the north. Although thrown around when the engagement started the young Germans, supported and strengthened by the hardened veterans of Operation Barbarossa, of the encirclement of Byalistock, of Minsk and of the march on Moscow, hung onto their positions. Attacking them were courageous fighters who ran at them shouting *"Hurrah"*; but German weapons from which spurted long red and yellow flames soon took a heavy toll of even the bravest of them. Enveloped in the smoke from all the shooting, his eyes streaming, Oberst Köhler soon saw the Russians retreating amid an appalling cacophony.

At the end of the day, 19. Pz.Div. overwhelmed Razumnoe, got hold of the cooperatives situated to the northeast of Generalovka and Yuroshaya, and then got ready to take Blishnaya Yigumenka. I./Pz.Gren.Rgt.74 from Kgp.74 was attached to Kgp Becker to facilitate the progress of their tanks. As for Kgp. 73, it was still committed to taking Kreida where the Russian resistance still did not waver.

Following Schmidt's division through the terrain it had captured, Generalleutant Chales de Beaulieu of 168 I.D. asked his Landsers to clear up any areas of resistance left behind by 19. Pz.Div. To avoid any confusion and to establish the best possible communication among the units, he had to avoid any movement within 19. Pz.Div.'s lines, and to keep in permanent contact with the 3. SS-Totenkopf Division and 7. Pz.Div.

But III. Pz.Korps' progress could not fail to attract General Watutin's attention, especially 7. Pz.Div. which had broken through his 7th Army's defences. He called up his reserves sending the 35th Guards Infantry Corps comprising the 92nd, 93rd and 94th Infantry divisions.

Below:
Sketch made by an artillery observer from Pz.Art.Rgt.19 which shows the zone where 19. Pz.Div. was engaged. From the outset, this division's main objective was to get hold of the heights situated near Blishnaya Yigumenka. The two towers of the station at Kreida where the Russian observers were hidden can also be seen. This town as only captured on 7 July 1943 by Kgp. 73 under Oberst Köhler with I./Gren. Rgt. 429. Köhler was killed during the afternoon when the town was attacked.
(After Rudolf Hinz. 19. Pz.Div.)

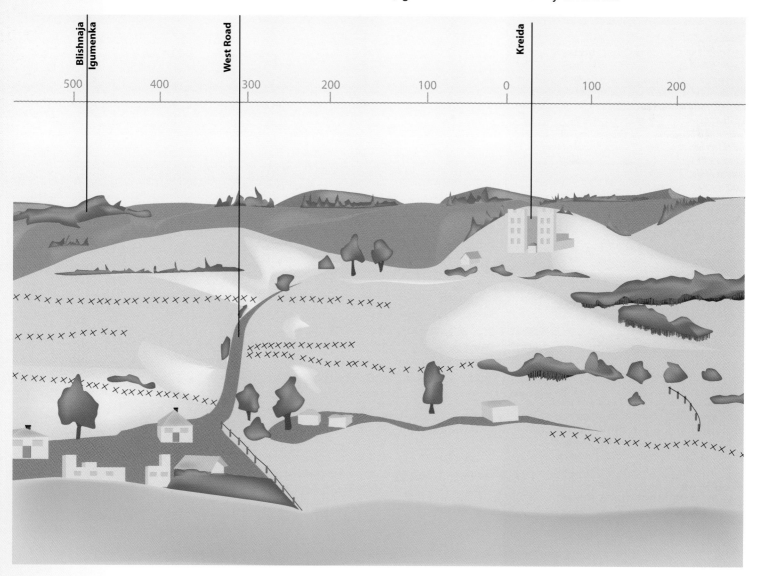

Above:
The Battle of Kursk usually evokes a gigantic tank battle. It must not be forgotten that 50% of the infantry regiments were horse-drawn, just as in the Battle of Normandy. For the 3 060 soldiers of an infantry regiment, there were 626 horses. This shot shows a Schützenkompanie moving up. The wagon in the foreground is being used to carry ammunition, witness the use of four horses instead of the usual two, like for instance with the following wagon which probably contains fodder.
(DAT 1939 L14)

Right:
Six horses were needed to draw the Protzwagen 18 (the ammunition limber) which is here pulling an l. FH 18. Driving such a team was difficult and did not allow for rapid movement or mobility. All the servers of the 15-cm gun rode a horse. The ordinary Artillery (on foot) no longer existed after WWI. This team is from a Geschützstaffel (artillery detachment) of a Gefectsbatterie (combat battery). Four of these detachments made up an artillery battery. The artillery regiment trucks bring up the rear of the column. A regiment of divisional horse-drawn artillery had a strength of 3 172 men, 2 208 horses, 240 carts of all types, 76 cars, 80 trucks, 57 motorbikes and 8 sidecars. (DAT 1939 L 16)

THE THIRD DAY OF THE OFFENSIVE: 7 JULY 1943

Generalfeldmarschall von Manstein clearly informed Gen. d. Pz. Tr. Breith that his three armoured divisions had to attack at the same time to progress northwards.

According to the plan, SS-Pz. Gren.Rgt. Das Reich, would continue to advance alongside 19. Pz.Div. which was to take the heights at Blishnaya Yigumenka, thus forming the far western end of the planned front line. This line went as far as Masikino Sabynino. 6. Pz.Div. remained in the centre of the disposition and on its right 7. Pz.Div. ensured that III. Pz.Korps' eastern wing was protected. VIII. Flieger-Korps would back up the attack with its Stukas.

THE 19. PZ.DIV. SECTOR

So as to keep luck on his side, Generalleutnant Schmidt had to protect his rear because the previous fighting had greatly weakened his division: it had advanced very quickly, leaving strongpoints in its wake which now had to be cleared up. At the outset this had been I.D. 168's job, but in the meantime this division had been ordered to take up defensive positions on the Donets. Its Gren. Rgt. 429 had been assigned to 19. Pz.Div. and had gone off towards Kreida which Kampfgruppe Köhler had to capture.

KAMPFGRUPPE 73

At 7.45, in an orgy of superhuman courage and savagery, Oberst Köhler's Panzergrenadiere deployed on either side of the railway line, rushing the Russian lines around Kreida station. They had dreaded this moment all night. They had been fighting for this group of buildings since the day before. It had already cost them the lives of several of their comrades. Their heads were filled with the racket of automatic arms fire and they let go of their highly-strung nerves by doing their grim job. In those moments there was no longer any mercy. All that mattered was saving one's own skin.

With the station now taken, Oberst Köhler arrived in his command car and encouraged his officers to invest Kreida itself. The town was covered in billowing clouds of black smoke. The Panzergrenadiere continued advancing, ready to tear apart any Russians who chose not to surrender. They rushed the fortified positions which they sprayed liberally with bullets. Men fell on both sides. Supplied with ammunition during the night, Köhler's soldiers

Above:
This fighter has crashed in a Russian village and is on fire. In spite of appearances, few pilots were killed during the Battle of Kursk. With a total of 27 221 sorties, the Luftwaffe lost 193 machines between 5 and 15 July 1943. To be more precise, VIII. Flieger Korps lost 99 machines for 14 398 sorties and 1. Flieger Division lost 94 for 12 283 sorties. The Russians lost almost a thousand planes.
(DAT 1937- L15)

poured streams of lead onto the enemy.

Less than thirty minutes later, the Russians fell back under fire from the machine guns and Oberstleutnant Goernemann's artillery.

At about 9 o'clock, Gren. Rgt. 429's infantry reached the first houses of Kreida in a long column. They forced a way through the smoking ruins with their horse-drawn carts; this was not without problems for the horses. On the way, they passed a first-aid post set up in a hangar where a doctor was looking after the wounded with the help of three nurses. There were about thirty of them. Nearby were parked two ambulances. Unfortunately some of the wounded could not be moved because of their wounds and they had to be left behind. Near the church forty or so well-guarded Russian prisoners were herded together. The booty was impressive: 45 machine guns, 29 mortars, three anti-tank guns, 80 rifles and ammunition.

The Panzergrenadiere guessed that something was amiss - the presence of these Landsers there was an ominous sign. Just enough time to smoke a cigarette, to down a quick glassful and they were off. Oberst Köhler led his men to the northeast. It was II./Pz.Gren.Rgt. 73 that took the first shots. The "*ratch boom*" of mortars, and Stalin's organs thundered their intense, frightening fire.

"*This barrage shows that we're close to a line of defence*", announced Oberst Köhler, "*they know we're going to attack so they're trying to break our strength.*"

A Leutnant ran up, bringing information from the Kdr. He was a liaison officer and he informed them where a trench bristling with machine guns was located. Oberst Köhler spent a long moment scrutinising the perfectly camouflaged trench with is binoculars. "*We will have to use our heavy weapons to clear out that position.*"

At the signal, the Panzergrenadiere bounded from their positions and swarmed all over the trenches. The support from the infantry's artillery turned out to be too formidable for the Russian heavy weapons which were shattered.

During this attack, a quarter of Köhler's strength was out of action before they had even reached the trenches and the Germans were outclassed by their opponents. It was an uneven struggle and Köhler ordered them to fall back.

They launched several attacks but each time these were shattered. At the end of the day, one of the companies only had ten men left. Pz.Gren.Rgt. 73 never got further than the woods to the north of Kolch.

The III. Pz.Korps diary mentioned: Kampfgruppe Köhler (Pz.Gren.Rgt. 73) suffered heavy losses during the heavy fighting. It was during the capture of the village of Blishnaya Yigumenka that the regiment's Kdr. was killed at the beginning of the morning.

One of the regiment's artillerymen tells

how Oberst Köhler fell on the field of honour. *"Once again, the areas of resistance caused a lot of casualties. The Grenadiere, whose ranks were getting thinner and thinner, rushed the Russian positions which we had spotted. They got hold of the first trench and were getting ready to throw themselves at the second when suddenly they came under fire from the infantry. We threw ourselves on the ground protecting ourselves with our spades while the bullets whistled around us, throwing up clouds of dust in the grass burnt dry by the sun. According to the regulations, I dug out a foxhole and sheltered. Soon sweat started streaming into my eyes and blinding me. A short while later, as I was moving backwards to set up radio con-*

Below Right:

A Grenadier has set himself in position behind a window. To be more at ease and be able to aim more calmly, he has got rid of his equipment and is sitting on an ammunition crate. His comrade is wearing a 1916-model helmet and carrying a 98 K of the same period. (BA 219/561/38)

Below left:

While a cloud of smoke rises above the burning fighter, two Landsers march through the deserted village streets. A year later, these soldiers were probably in the same situation in Normandy where the Allies lost as many men in three months as Army Group South did in July 1943.
(DAT 1937- L16)

tact, the Kdr. of Pz.Gren.Rgt.73, Oberst Köhler climbed out of a trench with two men and told me to give the order to fall back.

"The Russians stopped firing. Köhler brandished his knotted stick in the direction of an enemy bunker. There was the sound of a breach lock, immediately followed by a shot. Oberst Köhler was killed on the spot. I made my report and gave the Oberst's instructions."

Köhler's Panzergrenadiere had to continue fighting without their CO and obey the very demanding, if not suicidal, orders given by Major Horst who had taken over command from the dead colonel. Only this hard but fair officer's rigour could get them out of their predicament. This time, they had to clear a wooded area situated between Belovskaya and Blishnaya Yigumenka where the remnants of the Russian 81st Division were gathered. Once that mission was accomplished they headed for the heights situated more to the west where they set up defensive positions for the night.

THE BECKER KAMPFGRUPPE

With the help of the Stukas, II./Pz.Rgt. 27 and Pz.Gren.Rgt. 73, supported by I./Pz.Art.Rgt. 19, had to take Hill 215.5 overlooking Blishnaya Yigumenka. II./Pz.Rgt. 27's Panzer crews headed towards Hill 215.5 located to the northwest of Jastrebovo. Their 75-mm cannon thundered as soon as they spotted the anti-tank guns firing at them. The leading tank received a direct hit from an anti-tank gun fired at less than 60 yards. The shot blew a hole in the armour. The tank commander appeared, wounded and soaked in blood through the turret hatch and tried to get out.

The following tanks passed the wreck, and carried on their way without stopping to help the crew in difficulty. For some unknown reason when one of the Panzers tried to turn back it was run into by the following tank which then continued on its way.

A flash of light. A tremendous ball of fire and the monstrous thunder of the Apocalypse. A tank had been hit and a thick cloud of smoke billowed out all over the place. The sickening smell of diesel and burning flesh…

Despite starting in the most incredible chaos, I./Pz.Rgt. 27's tanks rushed the heights. This time the Panzerschutzen had things under control, just as if they were on exercise.

Shouts and orders in Russian from the heights were suddenly silenced by the shells as the Panzers began their barrage. Encouraged by this

precious support, the Panzerschutzen got nearer and nearer to the top of the hill. Their shooting intensified.

The ranks of the Russian 81st Division started to panic. They tried throwing grenades to get themselves out and fall back, but the terrible tank tracks inevitably caught up with them. It was no longer a fight but a slaughterhouse.

Oberst Becker had not smiled for two days. At last, his Kampfgruppe

Above:
Some Grenadiere have dug themselves into their foxholes near a wrecked T-34. It's lunchtime. The Gefreiter is eating from his mess tin while his comrade, the first machine gunner, remains at his post making jokes.
(BA 219/562/24)

had reached its objective. But he was not the Kdr. of an armoured regiment for nothing. All this was not enough for him. He drew up orders which he handed to his Melder (Translator's note: Messenger) who disappeared on his Zundapp in a cloud of dust.

Once he got the instructions, the Kdr. of I./Pz.Rgt. 27, Hauptmann Dietrich Willikens, gathered his company commanders together: *"We have to go very fast now to capture Hill 212.1 Take the initiative and be adaptable to the way things go. Enemy tanks and anti-tank guns are expecting you. We've got two cards up our sleeves. First, the presence here of Oberstleutnant Richter's Panzergrenadiere and second, surprise."*

At nightfall, Hill 212.1 was in their hands. However, the Russians were not going to admit defeat just like that. Groups of infantry supported by artillery got into position between Postnikoff and Delnazhaya Yigumenka.

To the west it was tanks and anti-tank units which came up into the line;

Top right: *Lying in the grass, this Feldwebel is scanning the countryside with his binoculars. He has been careful enough to place his 98K next to him.* (BA 219/562/28)

Left:
A large-calibre shell has hit this 1943-model T-34. Its ammunition has exploded under the impact, causing a terrible implosion which has ripped off the turret. Note the metal handles welded onto the hull and the turret, for the infantry to hang onto. (BA 220/630/4a)

on the banks of Dan Yuroshaya, Russian infantry was still digging itself in.

These were ominous movements for the men of Pz.Rgt. 27. When Oberst Becker reached Blishnaya Yigumenka with his two Abteilungen commanders, he found the place on fire. Here and there houses were burning. Becker presented himself to Oberstleutnant Richter, CO of Pz.Gren.Rgt.74. The latter's face was serious, his features haggard and drawn. He told him Oberst Köhler was dead. Several of his company commanders gathered round him waiting for orders. They knew that they had a lot of fighting ahead of them. With their greatly reduced numbers, they wondered when they were going to be relieved… This was an illusion since for III. Pz.Korps did not have any reserves at all.

"Gentlemen", announced Oberst Becker without beating about the bush, *"do not count on us for to night because the Russians have placed thousands of mines in front of us. They alone have the initiative since they know where to attack from. All that's left for you to do is to dig yourselves in where you are. As for me, I have to go and get ready to attack Melikhovo."*

Suddenly in the distance the officers of 19. Pz.Div. heard the dull thundering sounds of heavy motorised machines coming from the Russian lines.

Oberst Becker was mistaken in thinking that it was just his tanks which had to assemble to the northeast of Blishnaya Yigumenka; those from 6. Pz.Div. had to as well and it was almost midnight when the commanders learnt of these new dispositions.

As for the Grenadiere from 168 I.D. who were spread out fan-like in front of Staryzh Gorod, they had to set themselves up to the east of the Donets. This last movement of the corps meant that the strongpoint (Schwere Punkt) ordered by Gen. d. Pz. Truppen Breith had been established.

THE 6. PZ.DIV. SECTOR

In the centre of III. Pz.Korps's positions, 6. Pz.Div. under Generalmajor von Hünersdorff had to capture Yastrebovo

Right: Sappers opening the way for the tanks by clearing mines. Only one of these men seems to be equipped with a detector. Two others are searching for mines by prodding the ground with their bayonets. The Sapper on the left is wearing the combat uniform which was better suited to the heat than the thick woollen uniforms his comrades are wearing. As can be seen, the helmet cover was widely distributed by the time of the Battle of Kursk.
(BA 101 I 219/595/33)

Oberst Köhler was killed on 7 July 1943 when Blishnaya Yigumenka was captured. He was awarded the Knight's Cross on 27 July 1941 and the German Gold Cross.
(Photo J. Charita. Coll. D.L.)

and Sevriukino. It was von Oppeln Bronikowski's Panzerkampfgruppe which was given this mission.

At 4.30 Oberst von Oppeln Bronikowski set the objectives for his group of officers. An hour and a half later, they reached their starting positions.

At 7.30, the four operational Tigers under Hauptmann Burmester and the 7.Pz.Rgt. 11 led a column with air cover from Stukas. Not very far away, Oberst von Oppeln Bronikowski and his staff made sure things went off as planned. Soon Kampfgruppe Unrein (elements from Pz.Gren.Rgt. 4 of 6. Pz.Div.) joined up with these tanks to the north of Belinskaya. The Panzers progressed calmly.

Suddenly the Panzerschützen heard *"Achtung Minen"* shouted over the radio. The tanks ground to a halt. Hauptmann Burmester immediately called up the Sappers.

Fortunately, 3./Pz.Pi.Abt. 57 had been incorporated into the Panzergruppe. Some ten minutes later, the Sappers were at work. Unstintingly they defused the mines then threw them to either side of the corridor which they then marked out with strips of white cotton.

Once the path was safe, the crews got going again slowly then reached the outskirts of Sevriyukovo.

Still leading, Oberleutnant Reutemann of 7./Pz.Rgt. 11 went on ahead of the immobilised Panzergruppe to reconnoitre. Russian tanks placed on his right flank did not take long to react. The well-camouflaged anti-tank guns in turn opened fire and the company commander's tank took a direct hit. His Pz. IV miraculously continued to advance. Instead of getting away, the Panzer Oberstleutnant shot back at the enemy tanks. When the 7./Pz.Rgt. 11 crews spotted the Russian tanks chasing their CO, they started firing with their 75-mm cannon almost immediately.

"Don't worry about those tanks", shouted Oberleutnant Reutemann,

"Get to Sevriyukovo as quickly as possible."

In tight formation, his company's tanks rushed as fast as possible towards the village, churning up a huge cloud of dust which concealed them. The Russian tanks and anti-tank guns fired at the moving mass but nothing could stop it. Eight anti-tank guns were reduced to scrap and a T-34 got a direct hit.

At 11 o'clock, the 7th's CO announced to Oberst von Oppeln Bronikowski: *"Mission accomplished, Sevriyukovo is ours."*

The first obstacle the Panzergruppe met was getting across the Rasumnaya as both bridges had been destroyed by the Red Army and the fords were impossible to use. Sappers from the 3./Pz.Pi.Btl. 57 started work with the

help of the Pontoneers who had come up in support. They had to build a 24-tonne capacity bridge. But the enemy was quite decided not to let the Panzergruppe's tanks get through. The enemy artillery fired at the Sappers who stubbornly carried on working. Under a hail of projectiles, they hung on to their bridge, crouching in their foxholes, dug into the river banks. The shells exploding in clumps knocked the girders over. The whole sector became a living hell. The wounded Sappers were taken to the first aid post recently installed at Kolonozh-Dubovzh by a section of 57th Medical Company from 6. Pz.Div.

Oberst von Oppeln Bronikowski was furious. He called on II./Pz.Gren.Rgt.

114 to cover the Sappers with their fire. Equipped with SPWs, they were 6. Pz.Div.'s shock armoured infantry battalion. An hour later, the Panzergrenadiere built up a new bridgehead beyond the Rasumnaya.

The Russians furiously launched attacks to reduce the bridgehead but the German's iron grip held fast. The situation was critical. The Panzergruppe was constantly under a barrage of fire from the Russian artillery who were masters of the field. At the end of the morning, Oberst von Oppeln Bronikowski gathered all his armour together at Sevriyukovo: its northern sector was in danger.

When he was informed at 8 p.m. that the bridge was ready, von Oppeln Bronikowski immediately radioed an order the officers of his Panzerggruppe had already heard before: *"Get ready, we're crossing the Rasumnaya"*.

Without being able to say exactly when it took place during the offensive, the former Kdr. of s. Pz.Abt. 503 recalls the following episode which might well have taken place that very day. *"As I had*

to get in touch with 1./s. Pz.Abt. 503 which was out on a covering operation, I drove my Kübelwagen northeast. On the return, I thought I'd take a shortcut and find my way with the help of the sun. Thus with my driver I hurried down a defile. When the Ivans' artillery fire fell upon an escarpment about a mile and a half in front of us, I made a guess at the calibre.

"At the bottom of the depression, we followed a bend which took us to the right. There our hearts stopped beating. In front of us were ten Russian soldiers, most of them officers, talking in the middle of the sandy track. I shouted immediately: 'Step on it!' Surprised they jumped aside while we lowered our heads to avoid machine gun bullets. We expected to run into other Russian positions.

"Suddenly I spotted a German helmet just sticking out of the ground and a few yards further along we came a cross a forward unit of Panzergrenadiere belonging to a neighbouring division. We were safe and sound again".

THE 7. PZ.DIV. SECTOR

7. Pz.Div. advanced across terrain which was completely bare but nevertheless good enough for the Russian 31st Battalion to set up an ambush with its 7.62-cm anti-tank guns. Of all the armoured corps' divisions, 7. Pz.Div. was the one which advanced furthest into the enemy positions on 7 July. 1./s. Pz.Abt. 503 was still attached to it.

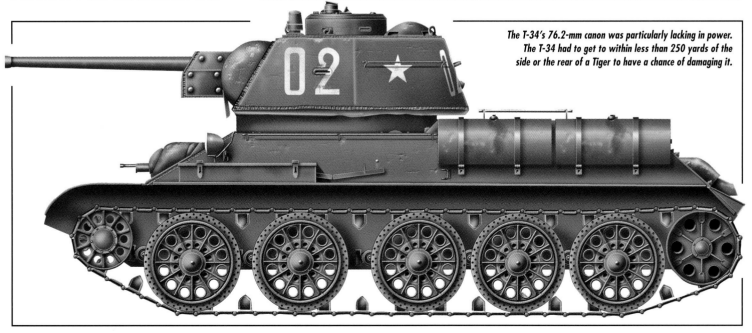

The T-34's 76.2-mm canon was particularly lacking in power. The T-34 had to get to within less than 250 yards of the side or the rear of a Tiger to have a chance of damaging it.

But the arrival of the 94th Guards Division unbalanced the eastern flank of III. Pz.Korps, and with it all the plans. In order to reinforce Pz.Rgt. 25, Gen. d. Pz. Tr. Breith called in the Tigers from 1./s. Pz.Abt. 503 then asked for I./Flak Rgt. 61 to be reinforced by II. Gr. from that regiment. V./Art.Reg. 248 remained attached to 7. Pz.Div.

As for the Tigers of 3./s. Pz.Abt. 503 (less the 2nd Section), they escorted II./Pz.Rgt. 25's Panzers to break up an attack by a Russian regiment. After repelling it, the tanks hurried off together to near the Miassoyedovo area, Pz.Gren.Rgt.7's objective.

Erich Seidel, a veteran from Pz.Gren.Rgt.7, who took part in the capture of this village, recalls: *"After a short time to get ready, we attacked this village which was situated in a valley. As I had had to take a message to the 3. Kp., I stayed with them. The Panzergrenadiere went on ahead.*

"There was very heavy fighting in that area. The Russian troops were dug in and they had to be got out yard by yard. The Russian artillery was firing for all it was worth when a salvo from Stalin's organs fell in the middle of a small group. We waited in open ground for

Centre:
Officers from s. Pz.Abt. 503 are eating near the village bombed by the Luftwaffe. From left to right: Hauptmann Burmester (1. Kp. CO), Leutnant Linden (ordnance officer) and Oberleutnant Scherf.
(© ECPAD DAT 3014- L11)

Opposite:
Unteroffizier Jäckel – Tiger 331 – following the bombing through his binoculars.
(© ECPAD DAT 3014- L15)

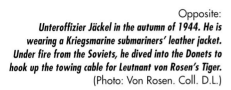

Oberleutnant Walther Scherf was born at Giessen. He was called up in November 1937 and put in the 8./Pz.Rgt. 1. He became a Leutnant in the reserve and a section commander in that company in April 1940. During the Campaign for France, he led the Reconnaissance Section of II ./Pz.Rgt. 1. He was awarded the Iron Cross, 1st and 2nd Class. He was hospitalised after being wounded at Pleskau in July 1941. He was then in the reserve battalion of Pz.Rgt.1. When he became an Oberleunant, he was ordered to go to Fallingbostel in April 1942 where he joined s. Pz.Abt. 502 which was being formed. This unit was engaged in December 1942 in the south of Russia. Oberleunant Scherf commanded the 2. Kp. A month later the company became the 3./s. Pz.Abt. 503. The next important step for Oberleutnant Scherf was when he led his company into battle during Operation Citadel. In October 1943, Scherf was awarded the German Gold Cross.

Since the Kdr. of s. Pz.Abt. 503 was absent, Walther Scherf had to replace him. This was why he was in command of the heavy battalion from the end of January to the end of February 1944, during which period his unit was attached to Panzergruppe Bäke which was ordered to break the Tcherkassy pocket. On 23 February 1944, he was promoted to Hauptmann and awarded the Knight's Cross.

When s. Pz.Abt. 503 was reformed, Hauptmann Scherf was again in command of 3. Kp. which was engaged during Operation Goodwood. Since he had to remain at headquarters, he delegated command of the unit to a young section commander, Leutnant von Rosen. After that operation, the company had to re-form and went to Mailly-le-Camp where it was given its new Tiger IIs. On his own initiative, Hauptmann Scherf decided to join the bridgehead at Mantes at the end of August 1944.

In September 1944, he went to the tank school at Bergen and was then required to command Kampfgruppe Y within Panzer-Brigade 150 under the famous Skorzeny. He took part in Operation "Greif" during the Ardennes offensive. In January 1945, he commanded s. Pz.Abt. 512 made up of Jagdtigers. Awarded the Ehrenblattspänge on 2 February 1945, he continued fighting in the Ruhr pocket and was finally made prisoner in April 1945.

(© ECPAD DAT 3014- L31)

Hauptmann Scherf wearing social uniform.

Hauptmann Walther Scherf on the day of his wedding. Leutnant von Rosen is in the background on the left.
(Photos: von Rosen. Coll. D.L.)

Below:
For ideological reasons, the Mathilda IIs, together with other American and British materiel, were very rarely presented in public. The ones that we do see were therefore photographed by German reporters who always show them as wrecks. These Mathilda IIs were engaged in large numbers during the Battle of Kursk, accompanying the infantry in the role for which they were designed. This British tank had its hour of glory at the beginning of the North African Campaigns (1941-1943). Its thick armour (78 mm) made it invincible except when it came up against German 88-mm guns. Subsequently outclassed by the Pz IIIs and Pz. IVs., it was delivered to the Russians according to the terms of the Lend-Lease where it turned out to be of little use against its adversaries. Its weak 40-mm canon and its slow speed (15 mph) left it little chance of survival.
(DR Caption by M. Chaubiron)

the explosions to end, lying on our stomachs in the dip caused by a ploughed furrow. Luckily the strident noise of the Stalin's organs covered the chaos. Two or three of our men were wounded.

"Bit by bit, in twos and threes we joined the assault troops who had reached the first houses. After taking up position, they went into the village and secured the entrance. The enemy was entrenched on a slope which they were holding onto very firmly. While we were digging in, snipers caused casualties in our company.

"Company HQ was located in the part of the church which was still solid. From the loft, we could see our soldiers in position lower down. On the other side we could clearly make out the bunkers and the Russian anti-tank guns. The reconnaissance group under Oberfeldwebel Christian Krämer climbed the slope under fire. Then they attacked the enemy at the same time throwing stick grenades and clusters of grenades held together with wire. The Russian foxholes and machine gun posts were the first to suffer. Through our binoculars, we watched the action develop.

"Everything inside the church was destroyed; despatch riders, radio operators, nurses, stretcher-bearers – everything and everyone belonging to a headquarters - were spread out in the corners of the building. The wounded were laid out on the beaten earth floor.

"Anti-tank gun and mortar shells

Feldwebel Karl-Heinz Rossbach,
2./Pz.Gren.Rgt. 7.
He was awarded the German Gold Cross on
30 July 1942 when an NCO with 6./SR and the
Knight's Cross on 6 June 1943 for bravery shown
at the head of his section during the fighting in the
winter of 42-43. He was still a section commander
in 2./Pz.Gren.Rgt. 7 during Operation Citadel. He
fell in battle in Italy on 25 February 1944.
(Photo J. Charita. Coll. D.L.)

Below:
This Panzer III command tank belongs to Major Bäke,
Kommandeur of the II./Pz.Rgt. 11 of the 6. Pz.Div. The insignia
on the left of the fronton is that of the 6. Pz.Div., the one on
the right is that of Oppeln von Bronikowski's group.

crashed onto the thick church walls which miraculously stood up to the bombardment. The despatch riders called for ammunition and the wounded cried to be sent to a first aid post.

"Suddenly officers from divisional headquarters turned up to get an idea of the situation for themselves and seemed quite dissatisfied with the way Operation Citadel as going.

"However that may be, our battalion had reached its objective, but with heavy casualties. A large number of anti-tank guns, mortars and machine guns had been destroyed and 200 prisoners belonging to a weakened supply unit had been taken. The pressure on the Landsers continued. Optimism was starting to fade away gradually".

General Shumilov of the 7th Guards Army had very skilfully got the units facing 7. Pz.Div. to withdraw so that it could progress deep into the Russian lines (this explains 7. Pz.Div.'s progress). Thus the divisions which remained in reserve now started to attack 7. Pz.Div.'s right flank.

XI A.K., whose main mission had been to protect the right flank of 7. Pz.Div., was held at bay - and for good - by the Russian 25th Corps' three infantry divisions.

Henceforth, 7. Pz.Div. not only had to protect its own threatened flank but III. Pz.Korps' flank too. This prevented it from being the spear head of the assault, a role which fell to 6. Pz.Div., since it now found itself in the centre of Gen. d. Pz. Tr. Breith's army corps.

Unteroffizier Gotthold Wünderlich was Hauptmann Scherf's tank driver throughout the whole war. Together they were in the 1. Pz.Div. during the campaign in the West in 1940. A year later, Wünderlich found himself at the gates of Moscow. Transferred to 3./s. Pz.Abt. 503 he continued as his Panzerfährer. After Operation Citadel, he fell back with the battalion in the direction of Merefa, Poltava, Kremenchug. When he was wounded he had to leave his post for four months. He fought for the Tcherkassy pocket. Back in France, he was engaged in the Battle of Normandy. In August 1944, aboard a Royal (Königs) Tiger, Wünderlich took part in the battle for the Mantes bridgehead. Hungary was his next assignment, then Abteilung "Y" in Skorzeny's Panzer-Brigade 150 in December 1944. After having driven almost every kind of tank he finished the war on a Jagdtiger. Captured by the Americans, he was freed in July 1945.
(Photo: Wünderlich. Coll. D.L.)

THE FOURTH DAY OF OPERATION CITADEL: 8 JULY 1943

Gen. d. Pz. Tr. Breith could well congratulate himself on the success of his concentric attack because his three armoured divisions had clearly progressed on the previous day. However, the danger arising from the breach in his left flank and that of II. SS-Pz. Korps was getting bigger and bigger. It now was some 20 miles wide and what Generalfeldmarschall von Manstein had feared from the beginning of the offensive would happen was actually taking place.

In order to remove this danger, 19. Pz. Div. would have to succeed in crossing the North Donets and appear suddenly in the rear of the 81st Guards Regiment which was busy fighting the 168 I.D. which itself was defending Belgorod and Staryzh Gorod. Generalmajor Chales de Beaulieu's infantry division took on the role of shock unit with the six assault guns of StuG. Abt. 228.

When he was faced with this situation, Gen. d. Pz. Tr. Breith wondered why the Russians did not take advantage of the breach separating his corps from II. SS-Pz. Korps.

Indeed General Watutin, Commander-in-Chief of the Voronezh Front and a great

STURMGESCHÜTZ ABTEILUNG 228

This battalion of assault guns formed up at Luckenwalde at the end of 1942. It consisted of three batteries and was created for use in North Africa; but at the last minute it was ordered to Russia. It got to Ostrov for Christmas where it was attached to the 8. Armee. It took part in the operations to break through the Russian lines and rescue the soldiers trapped inside Stalingrad.

StuG. Abt. 228 took part afterwards in the capture of Karkhov and the Battle of Kursk which were followed by several engagements when the Germans started to withdraw, the most noteworthy being those at Krementschug and Poltava. Its last great fight in Russia was for the Tcherkassy pocket.

As of 14 February 1944, StuG Abt. 228 became StuG. Brigade 228. It then fought in Romania and in Hungary where it suffered heavy losses. It played a determining role in the Gran Szolnok bridgehead then finally took part in rearguard action alongside the 15. I.D. in Austria. Its successive COs were: November 1942 to March 1944: Hauptmann von Malachowski, then Friedrich Moraw for the next two months then Hauptmann Rupert Knuppel until June 1944 then Hauptmann Kurt Teschke until the end of the war.

Red Army soldier, was particularly worried by the progress made by XXXXVIII. Pz. Korps which was threatening Obozhan. It is worth remembering that this town was only 32 miles to the south of Kursk. He was not worried by the rest of the front in particular since he had enough reserves to hold his lines.

The composition of a Sturmgeschütz Abteilung during Operation Citadel

Issued with Abteilung HQ
2 motorbikes
1 mot. Vehicle

HQ company
- Radio reconnaissance platoon
    1 Veh., 3 Pz. IIIs
- Engineer platoon
    1 motorbike
    3 veh.
- 4 reconnaissance sections
    2 motorbikes
    1 veh.
    1 platoon
- 3 Engineer sections
    1 SPW, 1 veh.
    1 platoon
- 1 Anti-Aircraft platoon
    1 motorbike, 4 veh.
    3 SPWs
    3 20-mm AA guns

Three companies
of Sturmgeschütze
Each company comprised:

Company HQ
3 motorbikes, 1 veh.
3 StuG IIIs
3 platoons of Sturmgeschütze
4 StuG IIIs

Total
StuG IIIs	42
Pz. IIIs	3
20-mm flak guns	3
SPW	6
Infantry platoons	4
Engineer platoons	3
Motorbikes	21
Vehicles	19

Right:
A Sturmgeschutz III belonging to StuG. Abt. 189 photographed several weeks before Operation Citadel started. It still has its protective side skirts which have been camouflaged. The rest of the machine has been covered with leaves. This battalion was engaged in the north pincer and was attached to the Sturm Division - XXIII A.K. (DR)

Hauptmann Wilhelm von Malachowski was in command of Sturmgeschütz Abteilung 228 from its creation until March 1944. He was born in Rostock on 6 June 1914. He joined the German army in 1935 and was put into Inf. Rgt. 27. Two years later he chose the artillery and joined the ranks of Art. Rgt. 48. When WWII broke out, he was Zugführer then Oberleutnant in 7.Art. Reg. 48. His unit took part in the Polish campaign then in the conquest of the Netherlands and France the following year. In 1940 he volunteered for the Sturmartillerie and was immediately transferred to Sturmgeschütz Abteilung 189. A year later he was in command of 2./Stg. Abt. 189. His battery and the two others in his battalion were ordered to support both infantry regiments of 110 I.D. They were engaged on 21 August 1941 to the west of Welikizhe Luki. The Sturmgeschütze threw themselves at the enemy positions from the very outset of the attack. They destroyed the wooden bunkers without any great difficulty then succeeded in forcing through the breaches in spite of marshy terrain which was sometimes mined. There were losses on the side of the Sturmgeschütze, most especially with the 3rd Battery which got stuck in the mud or drove over mines, and it was thus that Leutnant von Malachowski as wounded. However, the mission which 110. I. D. had been given - the capture of Welikizhe Luki - was successful. The commanders of both the army corps and the division paid tribute to StuG. Abt. 228 which had provided invaluable support to the Grenadiere. The same battalion was heavily engaged during the Battle of Wiasma-Briansk and at Kalinin. During the winter of 1941-42 to the north of Rshev, Oberleutnant von Malachowski and his battery distinguished themselves in a bitter struggle against the Russians who were threatening the bridgehead there. Where his assault guns were situated the fighting was endless. Not only did Malachowski have adequate firepower with his StuG. IIIs, but he used them with the right tactics.
On 30 January 1942, he was awarded the Knight's Cross and added a star to his shoulder flaps. He was a Hauptmann when he was designated to command StuG. Abt. 228 which was attached to one of the Heer's elite divisions: the Sturm Division - or rather 78. I.D.
On 1 March 1943, Malachowski was promoted to Major and awarded the Oak Leaves. Horribly tired by the strain of three years'fighting, Malachowski left his battalion and the 78. I.D. to teach what he knew to future officers at the Sturmgeschütze school at Burg. In May 1944 he taught at the Army armaments school; then from September 1944 to the end of the war, he was among senior officers on the Heer's General Staff. Wilhelm von Malachowski died on 28 October 1980. (Photo: J. Charita. Coll.: D.L.)

THE 6. PZ. DIV. SECTOR

This division progressed in quite a fantastic way even though it started badly during the first hours of the day.

Indeed, at 2 a.m., Panzerkampfgruppe von Oppeln Bronikowski crossed the 24-tonne bridge built the previous day by the Pioniere of Pz. Pi. Btl. 57 to join Kampfgruppe Unein.

When the Panzergruppe was up in the line ready to rush against Melikhovo at 6 o'clock, Oberst von Oppeln Bronikowski was given a last-minute counter-order.

The attack was put back by one hour because the mortar battalion which should have been in place for the start of operations was still being moved up.

At 7 o'clock, Oberst von Oppeln Bronikowski started cursing: there was still no news of the support battalion. He waited for another thirty minutes or so. Dawn was already breaking. Fearing that the Russians might take the initiative, he ordered his officers to attack.

Once again, 7./Pz. Rgt. 11 was the first to attack Melikhovo. It led the way

At the age of 16 he took part in the last year of WWI. He was a Major and assigned to the HQ of XI A. K. when he was recruited again for the Polish campaign of 1939. He was awarded the Iron Cross, Second class.

A few months later, he commanded Aufklärungs-Abt. 268. It was at the head of this unit that he was took part in the Netherlands and French campaigns which got him the Iron Cross, First Class. A short while later he joined the High Command Staff where he was assigned to the medal award service. A year later he was in 6. Pz. Div. in which he commanded a battalion of motorbikes (Kradschutzen Abt. 6) which he led to the gates of Moscow. He was then awarded the German Gold Cross. On 1 July 1942 he was at the head of Pz. Gren. Rgt. 4 and promoted to Oberst.

There followed a period of terrible fighting for the 6. Pz. Div., one of the divisions assigned to try and free the 6. Armee encircled in Stalingrad. Its Pz. Gren. Rgt. 4 struggled without letting up until April 1943. Once again the qualities of its commanding officer were rewarded; he was awarded the Ehrenblattspange. Once again his unit was used, this time for Operation Citadel. The fighting continued until September 1943. Oberst Unrein was awarded the Knight's Cross. The commands he was given were increasingly important: he took over the 14.Pz. Div. with the rank of Generalleutnant which got him his Oak Leaves. Then he took command of III. SS-Pz. Korps, the Panzerdivision "Clausewitz", until he was captured in April 1945. He spent more than ten years in captivity with the Soviets. He died on 6 January 1972.

(Photo J. Charita. Coll. D.L.)

Below:

The tank commander of this other Sturmgeschütz from StuG. Abt. 189 saluting the officers from divisional headquarters, probably 78 I.D.'s, as he passes them. The scene took place during training. (DR)

for the 5., 8. and 6./Pz. Rgt. 11 with Pz. Art. Regt. Jahn close on its heels. StuG. Abt. 228's assault guns brought up the rear. All these units were placed on the left wing and advanced together with 19. Pz. Div.

The flame-thrower tanks and the lighter vehicles remained in reserve for the time being.

As soon as the Panzers left, Kampfgruppe von Bieberstein, placed on the right wing, followed a river that led to Melikhovo. Kampfgruppe Unrein was in the centre of the attack.

At 8.45, 6. Pz. Div. found its progress blocked by a huge minefield from behind which Russian artillery thundered. Then anti-tank guns tried to take out the Panzers in von Oppeln Bronikowski's Panzergruppe.

7./Pz. Rgt. 11 was stopped in its stride and very shortly afterwards a storm of fire fell on the Panzers. They found themselves the target of a bombardment according to all the rules by the artillery and Stalin's organs set up near Postnikoff and Kalinina.

The Pioniere had to intervene to get them out of this predicament. They traced a safe passage through the minefield and the tanks were able to resume their mad charge. Towards 10 o'clock, they ran into an anti-tank ditch which blocked their approach to the town, only 2 _ miles away. As usual it was the Pioniere who got them over the obstacle by blowing up the edges of the ditch in order to flatten it out. This operation lasted three hours. Hardly had they recovered from this dangerous job than the Panzers rushed up to make use of the way through.

Two minefields halted their advance again. Operation Citadel was developing with dramatic intensity. The Panzerschützen were beginning to feel that they were never going to get the better of these defences.

Major Bäke's men took part in a sort of nightmare show. With all the concentration needed for such a task the Pioniere were crouching over the mines they were defusing. From time to time one of them dropped dead, with a bullet through his head. These shots came in particular from the trenches situated behind the minefields where Russian infantry were hiding in ambush.

Suddenly the sappers spotted SPWs coming in their direction crossing the open ground without even seeking shelter. The rubber tank tracks dug ruts in the sandy soil and threw up very heavy clouds of dust. This convoy was none other than Kampfgruppe von Bieberstein

Left: *One of 1./s. Pz. Abt. 503's crew looking at one of the half-tracks and Panzergrenadiere getting down from it.* (BA 22/2949/24)

Top left: *The commander of this Tiger has stopped his tank. The barrel points threateningly up towards the vast plain from which the enemy can suddenly start shooting. Two soldiers have been sent forward to reconnoitre on foot. They can be seen in the wheat field on the right going back to their half-track.* (BA 22/2949/22)

Top right: *This driver has nodded off during the break, leaning on his seat. The crews very often had to sleep in their tank and they even allowed themselves a short nap during the long hours waiting. The direction finder and the gyroscope are on the driver's left and the dashboard is on the right, out of sight on this photograph. The episcope for surveying the terrain can be seen clearly here.* (BA 22/2949/19)

Above: *Insignia of the Sturmgeschütze Abteilung 228. A large T replaced this insignia when the battalion became a brigade on 1 July 1944.* (Source: Schmitz/Thiez – Die Truppen Kennzeichen 1939-45)

Below: *Two Panzergrenadiere run from under cover and shelter behind mounds of earth. The armoured infantry turned out to be invaluable for accompanying the tanks. The two soldiers here have to spot the enemy who is probably lying in ambush somewhere.* (BA 22/2949/26)

Above: *The reconnaissance by the two Panzergrenadiere has paid off. They have managed to spot Russian anti-tank guns. Forewarned by radio, one of four Sd Kfz. tank busters from 1./Pz. Jg. Abt. 41 of 6. Pz. Div. intervenes. This self-propelled gun mounted on a Panzerkampfwagen 38 (t.) chassis opened the way for the Tigers. It had a 75-mm Pak 40/3 canon. This Pz. Jg. Abt. was also equipped with 7.62-cm Marder IIs and IIIs. Only two 7.62-cm Marder IIIs were destroyed during the Battle of Kursk (15 July). On 22 July some Sd Kfz 138s repelled a powerful Russian attack, destroying several tanks. As at 12 August 1943, the four machines were still with the company.* (BA 22/2949/28)

moving up. When they were at the right distance, the Panzergrenadiere opened fire with their heavy machine guns. They overtook the sappers and the sector that had just been cleared, then jumped down from their half-tracks and rushed the enemy positions.

Needless to say all this slowed the Panzers down considerably and in spite of the sappers' care, several of them ran over mines, thus reducing the armoured Abteilung's strength.

Given Kampfgruppe von Oppeln Bronikowski's delicate situation, Generalmajor von Hünersdorf contacted Generalleutnant Schmidt of 19. Pz. Div. He wanted his tactical group (probably Richter's Kampfgruppe) to be attached to him so that he could get hold of Melikhovo with the support of Pz. Rgt. 27. However they had to take into consideration the fact that they only had 15 tanks including the recently arrived replacements.

Towards 5 p.m., Pz. Rgt. 27 and 2./s. Pz. Abt. 503 rejoined von Oppeln Bronikowski's armoured group. Generalmajor von Hünersdorf insisted on commanding personally the reconnaissance units going off to report on the state of the Melikhovo defences. When he returned with enough information, this indefatigable General launched 5. And 8./Pz. Rgt. 11 at the western part

of the village. As for the Tigers of 1./s. Pz. Abt. 503, they opened the way for Pz. Gren. Rgt. 4 in the central sector.

Hünersdorf then asked Oberst von Bieberstein to join him as quickly as pos-

Geschützführer and NCO Hans Burbach from 2./Pz. Jg. Abt. 41 was awarded the Knight's Cross on 18 November 1943. (Photo J. Charita. Coll. D.L.)

sible with his unit. But the unit was trapped in front of Kalinina by the artillery barrage from the Russians situated on the heights at Miassoyedovo and was not exactly in a position to capture that village. The regiment had suffered so many casualties that it was going to have to be reorganised.

The armoured assault started under the cover of divisional artillery with two successive barrages. Flak Abteilung 34's cannon had a field day taking out the swarms of Russian fighters which attacked the advancing Panzers.

Oberst von Oppeln Bronikowski evokes this engagement which lasted two and a half hours: *"The attack started with Major Doctor Bäke's armoured battalion placed in the centre. But it wasn't long before he came across enemy infantry blocking his path. Fortunately they were swept aside by our explosive shells. Then Russian tanks approached.*

"Once again Major Bäke led his tanks with great skill. The battle started and already the enemy was already retreating. The Panzers destroyed two Russian tanks. In all, the two armoured groups destroyed 26 Russian tanks and the day's objective was reached."

Although Oberst von Oppeln Bronikowski's narrative is all to the credit of his regiment and in particular of Major Dr Bäke, he does leave out certain details like the virulent defence by a T-34 unit dug in up to the turret which suddenly revealed itself; or an infantry regiment, sheltering in trenches protected by barbed wire which kept up sustained fire at Oberst von Oppeln Bronikowski's armour and broke their charge.

Nevertheless Panzergruppe Becker, situated on Major Bäke's flanks, reacted efficiently since it destroyed 18 tanks and three half-tracks (afterwards claimed by Oberst von Oppeln Bronikowski). Hauptmann Burmester's Tigers destroyed the other tanks.

Dr Lochmann, a veteran of 1./s. Pz. Abt. 503, recalls: *"Although we destroyed all sorts of targets, we had to face those anti-tank guns which were set up in terrible defensive belts. There were so many of them that they gave me permanent diarrhoea. I had to get out every thirty minutes to satisfy my needs. Hiding behind the muzzle cover, I squatted down at the rear of the tank without the enemy noticing me. As well, it was dreadfully hot inside the Tiger and this made us constantly thirsty."*

A second armoured assault was launched. In thirty minutes, the infantry regiment was swept aside and 26 Russian tanks were knocked out all across the tortured landscape. Major Bäke's leading Panzers entered Melikhovo at exactly 4 p.m.

They took the town with the invaluable help of Pz. Rgt. 27 from 19. Pz. Div. attacking from the southwest but this was not without heavy casualties and clearing up operations were finally completed at about 6 o'clock the following day. 6. Pz. Div. set up a defensive line in a semi-circle to the north and the east of the town.

Capturing Melikhovo was not as simple as Oberst von Oppeln Bronikowski maintained. His regiment claimed some hits which belonged strictly speaking to 1. and 2./s. Pz. Abt. 503 which destroyed six T-34s inside the town. The number of Russian tanks destroyed by Pz. Rgt. 27 is unfortunately not known.

Meanwhile the Pioniere from 6. Pz. Div. fought off the Russian tanks attacking along the Belgorod – Korotscha axis with determination.

It is worth noting how important Pz. Art. Rgt. 76 was in its covering role. When the divisional artillery's CO, Oberstleutnant Grunherr, made a tally of enemy guns destroyed, he got the surprising total of 15 batteries.

Except for 6. Kp., all Major Bäke's II./Pz. Rgt. 11 was ordered to keep up

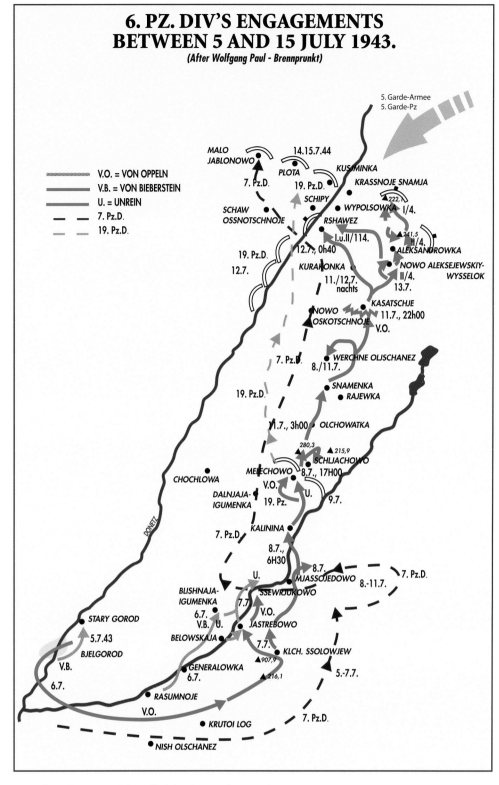

6. PZ. DIV'S ENGAGEMENTS BETWEEN 5 AND 15 JULY 1943.
(After Wolfgang Paul - Brennprunkt)

its effort by attacking Schlachovozhe from the west and on the way, to weaken Russian resistance in the northwest part of Melikhovo; they were then to take the Delnazhaya Yigumenka – Schlachovozhe road and go to point 220. 5./Pz. Rgt. 11 would cover the Abteilung's left wing.

Oberst von Oppeln Bronikowski waited for news of his unit in his headquarters command post hidden in the woods to the west of Melikhovo.

The Panzergruppe's progress was stopped by the unexpected presence of a new Russian infantry regiment: Colonel A.F. Vasiliyev's 305th from the 69th

Army reserve. This division was deployed along a defensive line including Shliakovo.

The 6. Pz. Div. campaign log stipulated that *"On 8 July, 6. Pz. Div. destroyed six tanks, 19 anti-tank guns and two trucks. About a hundred soldiers were killed and 130 taken prisoner"*. After taking part in the capture of Melikhovo, Pz. Rgt. 27 under Oberst Decker positioned itself to the northeast of Delnazhaya Yigumenka for the night, thus covering 6. Pz. Div.'s left wing. The Russians set up new positions to the northeast of Yuroshaya, not very far from Becker's Panzers.

THE 7. PZ. DIV. SECTOR

Generalmajor von Funck's division could not follow 6. Pz. Div. because 106.I.D. on its east wing was late joining them. As a result, the right flank was exposed and elements of Pz. Rgt. 25, supported by Tigers from von Rosen's section, had to defend it by occupying the heights situated some 2 miles to the southeast of Miassoyedovo.

Von Rosen, the veteran ex-Leutnant, recalls: *"We found ourselves on a slope with Panzers from I./Pz. Rgt. 25. I had been ordered to protect the regiment's position with my four Tigers to the east. So I positioned myself with two Tigers on a hill which allowed me to see eve-*

Below:
With the Panzerjäger leading, the second section of the 1st Company of the 503rd advances cautiously across the plain. The Russians, who are probably entrenched at the edge of the wood, have targeted one of the four Tigers. The tank tracks visible in the foreground, on the right of the photograph most certainly belong to the Panzergrenadiere's half-track. The reporter is with them. (BA 22/2949/22a)

rything and to open fire in case of attack.

"There was an escarpment In front of me with several dips separated by bushes. At the bottom of the valley, there was a very dense, half-moon shaped forest and far away on my left the plain spread out as far as the eye could see. The air shimmered in the heat.

"The two Panzers were joined by the section's other tanks and spent four hours on guard like that. We were finally able to wash. The water supply was very limited but there was enough for all the crew. Later we usually washed our hands with petrol. The night was calm."

Without any transport vehicles, Generalleutnant Forst's 106.I.D. could not even envisage being at the departure point in support of 7. Pz. Div. for the attack planned for 8 July in the morning. The latter division's strength had been considerably reduced since Operation Citadel was launched.

The Kdr. of XI.A.K., Gen. d. Pz. Tr. Raus asked for his corps to be reinforced because his two infantry divisions

could not hold out much longer on the Donets against the assaults of the Russian 7th Guards Army. Defending this position was all the more compromised as the Russians had launched the 15th Guards Division and an anti-tank battalion against 106. I. D. which for a while was supported by Pz. Rgt. 25 under Oberstleutnant Schültz. Reinforcements from 168.I.D. were promised as soon as possible. This infantry division had arrived the previous day by train and had to reinforce 7. Pz. Div.'s right wing.

With no longer any support on its east flank, Generalmajor von Funck's 7. Pz. Div. was not able to advance. It had to be content with following the River Razumnoe behind which it set up its positions and from which it was able to protect 6. Pz. Div.'s right wing.

THE 19. PZ. DIV. SECTOR

The Kampfgruppe Becker soldiers had fought all night. From the first moment of the attack they had been driven back by sustained fire from anti-tank guns and dug-in tanks from near the woods situated to the north of hill 212.1. Oberst Becker's command post received the following message *"Impossible to advance further, Colonel"*.

Half an hour later the German batte-

Right:
Russian pilots appreciating a moment's relaxation in front of a Yak. (DR Caption by M. Chaubiron)

Below:
Direct hit! An 88-mm shell has torn the turret off this T-34/76 off. The impact can be seen on the right of the turret. During the Battle of Kursk what the Red Army's arsenal did not have was a canon capable of piercing the Tiger's and Panther's armour plating at long range. The Russian tanks had to get as close at 250 yards to their targets to be sure of destroying them - which of course was suicide because the German crews naturally spotted the enemy well before he got into range. There was an 85-mm canon, but the T-34 could not take the weight.
(BA 220/630/3a*)*

ries went into action. A deluge of shells fell upon the Russian positions. A short while later, the Panzers from Pz. Rgt. 27 overwhelmed the last Russian defences. They continued their attack towards Kalinina but had to stop on the way. The ground was littered with mines. They waited impatiently for the sappers to come up. Several Panzerschützen fell asleep. But not for very long because less than an hour later, they were awoken by the on-board radio announcing *"Panzer Marsch!"*

The Panzers started off along the narrow tracks taped out by the engineers then came out in front of another Russian line of defence where the enemy showed it was just as stubborn. Amid the clattering tracks of Pz. Rgt. 27's Panzers and beneath a storm of fire and steel, Becker's men shattered the enemy's resistance.

But there was still a long way to go to Kalinina. Dawn was hardly breaking when 3-tonne Opel Blitz lorries from the supply train met up with the armour to fill their tanks. These men from the rear service areas ran just as great a danger as the front-line soldiers. They were often the targets for Russian fighters which spotted them as soon as they made the slightest movement.

A wind of terror seemed to blow over 19. Pz. Div. after the disappearance of Oberst Köhler; it was now the Kdr. of Pz. Rgt. 27 who was seriously wounded. He had to be taken as quickly a possible to the first aid post set up at Pavlovka. Nurses from the 9th Medical Company arrived later to take him to hospital in Tomarovka where he died a month later.

A young officer from the armoured units called Westhoven was given temporary command of Pz. Rgt. 27 or rather the Panzergruppe, which could now no longer scrape together more than 15 tanks, less than a company's normal strength. Finally command of the regiment fell to Oberst Hohmann on

Above:
Without doubt, this KV1 belongs to a unit of the Guard as the turret insignia (unfortunately not very legible) would seem to indicate. It is being followed by a BT7 tank which was completely out of date at the time of the Battle of Kursk.
(DR Caption by M. Chaubiron)

10 August 1943.

There was brief, harsh fighting at the beginning of the afternoon when the Panzers moved along the trenches firing with all their guns. Hit by the tank's machine guns, many Russian infantrymen just fell back in to their trenches.

The new Kdr. used all that he had to get the Russians out of the trenches including flamethrower tanks. The Russians realised the danger and broke off the engagement, withdrawing behind the woods where they re-formed.

Soon with rumbling engines, Wes-thoven's Panzers approached the anti-tank positions. The Russians tried to stop them but the 75-mm shells soon knocked out their positions.

The whole line of defence was on fire. Suddenly men with bazookas ran up with their long tubes, accompanied by infantry firing burst after burst at the Panzers with their automatic weapons; the Panzers on-board machine guns cut whole swathes through the ranks of infantry who fell all over each other, like dislocated puppets. With a horrifying noise, the Pz. IIIs and IVs knocked over, twisted and crushed the anti-tank guns. Splinters of steel flew up into the burning air.

Once calm returned to the valley, the Panzerschützen allowed themselves a short break. Westhoven scrutinised the countryside through his binoculars. He was the only one to remain in his tank. Standing up to his waist in the turret, he said: *"We haven't won yet! We've still got to take Kalinina."* Nobody moved. Two soldiers sent out to reconnoitre came back and told him that there was a minefield right in the way of their advance. The sappers had to intervene once again to open up a passage for the armour so that it could continue its mission.

Westhoven's Panzergruppe was atta-ched to 6. Pz. Div. for the capture of Meli-khovo, the day's main objective (as seen in the paragraph on the 6. Pz. Div.).

While Westhoven's tanks were strug-gling to the north of Hill 212.1 at first light, Oberstleutnant Richter's Pz. Gren. Rgt.74 broke the bristling first line of defence by destroying all the bunkers that covered it.

As soon as machine gun bursts got the better of the last spasms of resis-tance, Oberstleutnant Richter regrou-ped his men then launched an attack against the Russian defences set up on the edge of the woods to the north of Belovskaya. The operation was over quickly.

Their next fight was waiting for them in the heart of a hilly area, whose defen-ders clearly had the intention of han-ging on to each hill whatever the cost.

The Pz. Gren. Rgt.74 companies laun-ched attack after attack to get nearer these hills, but the number of casualties was very high. Because they were rus-hing over open ground, they dived

With its 43.5 tonnes, the KV-1A was the heaviest tank in the Soviet arsenal at Kursk. The later B version had a turret reinforced with extra plates of armour which weighed it down a further four tonnes.

behind bushes or into bomb craters, letting off a couple of shots at a time before leaping forward once more.

Oberstleunant Richter hurried his troops on. There was no other way. "*Faster, lads, faster*", he shouted into the radio after snatching the microphone from his operator under cover with him in a dip in the land. From time to time he watched on helplessly as several of his Panzergrenadiere leapt into the air, thrown up by exploding mines then falling back to the ground, ripped apart, horribly mutilated. The noise from the weapons and the explosions smothered the death cries of the wounded that could not be rescued and cared for until the heights were taken.

When they reached the foot of the last hill to be captured, the Panzergrenadiere got pinned down. Jumping aboard an SPW from his regiment's motorised company, Oberstleutnant Richter joined his men. He jumped from the vehicle and grabbed an incendiary grenade from a Feldwebel who was too shocked by the events. Richter set the example by throwing the grenade in the direction of the Russians who were firing continuously. The phosphorus sparkled and streamed over a machine gun nest.

Leading his group on, the Kdr. started climbing the grassy slope with trees of all sorts everywhere. Bullets and shrapnel flew all over the place. Smoke created dark, opaque screens in places and the din of the explosions was thrown back along the valley by the echo. The Panzergrenadiere rushed on until they ran out of breath. Only 200 yards more to go! Concentrating on these greenish targets who were rushing at them, the Russian infantry failed to spot that a company was creeping up behind them.

This company, when it had finished off the resistance on the eastern flank of the hill, raked machine gun fire down on the Russian infantry which was crushed in only a few minutes.

The shooting finally ceased. The Panzergrenadiere were out of breath. Their faces were black from the smoke and their uniforms were covered with a thick layer of dust. Their staring eyes said a lot for the tension and stress they had

just been through. "*Well done, lads, we've cleared the hill,*" Richter shouted pointing to a trench filled with Russian dead. *"There's nothing left here but the dead and the dying!"*

The Oberstleutnant turned to his adjudant and said: *"Now, call up the Scouts and have them occupy these positions we've taken. God alone knows when the Russkis will come back!"*

Major Wilmsen's Scouts did not come up as quickly as Oberstleutnant Richter expected. They were attached to Kampfgruppe 73 which was deemed too weak to carry out its mission. Indeed

now it barely had the strength of the equivalent of two companies. Kampfgruppe Richter did not have many more men either. When they put all the remaining troops from the two Panzer Grenadier Regiments in 19. Pz. Div. together they had only the equivalent of a battalion, at most.

At 10.30 exactly while Major Horst's Panzergrenadiere were fighting in front of the trenches to the east of Blishnaya Yigumenka, the Scouts reached the enemy's right wing. Two NCOs in command of a mortar section and a machine gun section put heart into the servers

The Russians also used a few German vehicles, like these Panzer III and IVs, in special units.
(DR - Caption by M. Chaubiron)

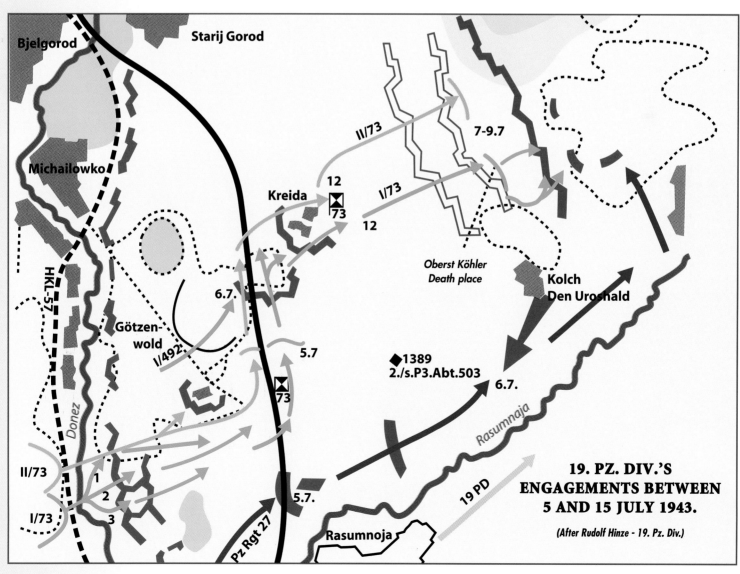

Bjelgorod

Starij Gorod

Michailowko

HKL-57

Donez

Götzen-wold

I/492

6.7.

Kreida

II/73

12
73
12

I/73

7-9.7

*Oberst Köhler
Death place*

Kolch
Den Uroshald

◆1389
2./s.P3.Abt.503

6.7.

5.7.

73

5.7.

II/73

1

2

I/73

3

Pz Rgt 27

Rasumnaja

19 PD

**19. PZ. DIV.'S
ENGAGEMENTS BETWEEN
5 AND 15 JULY 1943.**

(After Rudolf Hinze - 19. Pz. Div.)

Rasumnoja

of these back-up weapons. Major Horst's men managed to advance despite the machine gun fire and reached the innermost part of the enemy trench system. The Scouts did not take long to join them. The fighting turned out to be very savage. The bunkers were demolished and a great number of Russian soldiers lost their lives in this fighting. In spite of everything, the survivors bravely continued to resist in certain areas. The Scouts, badly shaken by the heavy arms fire, saluted their adversaries with machine guns bursts before they broke off and went south to set up defensive positions in front of Blishnaya Yigumenka.

Major Horst's soldiers were therefore in place when Generalleutnant Schmidt was ordered to take Blishnaya Yigumenka. It was difficult for him to comply because his units were already all in the front line and his armoured regiment had been attached to 6. Pz. Div.

A quick report was sent to Gen. d. Pz. Tr. Breith who could only think of one solution: solve the problem with Generalmajor de Beaulieu.

The 168.I.D. gave this mission to Gren. Rgt. 442 which left Jastrebovo in order to go over to the attack during the afternoon. The Grenadiers were surprised to find positions which had been well set up, with trenches, shelters and foxholes.

The intelligence service forgot to signal the Kdr. of the 442nd that a Russian infantry battalion had come up in support the previous night and that it had set itself up in new positions.

The Grenadiere had only just invested half the town when a counter-attack by a unit approaching the strength of one Russian regiment fell upon them. They got under cover as best they could to escape from all the shells which were falling nearer and nearer.

The pressure became such that the Grenadiere broke off the engagement in the southern part of the town under the weight of Russian fire. They thought their lungs were going to burst. Some rearguard elements managed to delay the enemy a few minutes at most by firing off a few bursts before running to catch up with their comrades.

The battalion and company commanders, often without any communication links managed to set up defensive positions. Although their positions were particularly perilous, the Grenadiere felt safer in this part of the town.

Generalleutnant Schmidt tried to set up permanent links with his units in order to maintain a continuous front. But it was extremely difficult for his subordinates who were under fire to get in contact when they arrived in sight of the heights to the north of Yuroshaya.

As for 168. I.D., it been under a Russian artillery barrage ever since the previous evening. When the cannon fell silent it was the heavy mortars which took over instead particularly in the Mikhailovka bridgehead sector.

The Landsers in the Gren. Rgt.417 under Major Barkmann set up new positions along the east bank of the Donets. The heavy company from Pz. Jg. Abt. 417 under Oberleutnant von Jordan supported them. Russian tanks had been spotted in the Tarnovka sector by air reconnaissance and were undeniably heading for the Belgorod-Kursk road. Meanwhile the Russian infantry started to move between Staryzh Gorod and Delnazhaya Yigumenka.

All these movements were not lost on

DOCUMENTARY REPORT THE FRONTLINE RADIO OPERATOR

His campaign radio slung over his shoulder, this Sprecher (Speaker) had to set up a signals relay between a company and its battalion. The headphones were placed in the right-hand section of the case.
(BA 198/1395/3a)

Above: *At a run, the Sprecher joins his comrade sheltering in a large hole. He is holding his helmet in his left hand and his 98K in his right. In order to relieve his already heavy-laden back, he has removed his helmet which he is holding in his left hand. Indeed the Sprecher had to carry the radio itself which weighed 30 lb together with 4 lb gasmask.* (BA 198/1395/7)

Top right: *The Sprecher and the Gefreiter liaise with the rear next to a Feldwebel armed with an MP 40 and decorated with the infantry insignia. The Sprecher can now relay information which may turn out to be useful or even important for the fighting. The radio had a maximum range of 0.6 mile.* (BA 198/1395/8a)

Below left: *While the Gefreiter is drinking from his flask, the Feldwebel keeps an eye on the landscape, his features marked by stress and tension. Note that the Sprecher has been decorated with the insignia awarded to the wounded.* (BA 198/1395/14)

Below right: *Some distance away another Sprecher has signalled the servers of some 81-cm mortars that he has succeeded in contacting the radio pair who have given him some details about the enemy positions. Already a shell has been stuffed into the barrel of the Granatwerfer as can be seen.* (BA 198/1395/24)

Above:
But the telephone link is not very good. While waiting for the line to be reconnected, the two soldiers refresh themselves. The depth of the valley in which is in front of their position is truly impressive. (BA 198/1395/12)

Right:

This long column of Russian prisoners is walking to the rear of the III. Pz. Korps. According to Generlfeldmarschall von Manstein, Army Group South captured 34 000 soldiers, killed 12 000 others and wounded 34 000 between 5 and 18 July 1943.
(BA 22/2925/05)

the 168. I.D. observers who had a lot to do. Their main tasks were to get rid of any pockets of resistance which had been left behind once the armour from 19. Pz. Div. had passed on its way, and to take over the captured positions. But the Landsers did not always get there on time and the Russians sometimes got there first. It was thus that the plateau and the heights were re-occupied by the enemy, particularly those at Glavplodoavitch, where more than two companies settled in after Becker's Panzers had left; and those situated a mile from Andreievski.

It was 2 p.m. when the Landsers from Gren. Rgt. 429 left Kreida and followed the railway line. They went through the station which had been taken the previous day by Kampfgruppe 73. The railway line delimited Major Vollmary's II. and III. Battalions. Their mission was to take Staryzh Gorod. The Grenadiere, exhausted by the fighting and overloaded with equipment and weapons, started marching again in silence. They sunk into sombre, nostalgic thoughts. For three days now they had been fighting on empty stomachs without sleeping, drinking tepid water from their water flask and eating stale bread. As the sun started to go down, they arrived in sight of Staryzh Gorod, held by the 81st Guards Infantry Division.

At the southern entrance to the town, the fighting was merciless. For a quarter of an hour, groups of machine gunners fired mercilessly at the Russian positions, spraying any of the enemy which dared show itself with bullets. Finally the Landsers succeeded in slipping through the breaches and advanced towards the houses relying more on instinct and praying they would not come under fire from the Russian Maxims and PPSHs.

Leading the way, Major Vollmary got his bearings in this hostile town where death roamed freely. Soon he was in radio contact with the CO of the 2nd battalion which had stayed in reserve; he ordered him in turn into action and to strike the enemy from the rear.

Suddenly like an echo, explosions echoed in the western part of the town. Shots crackled and MGs emptied belt after belt… The CO of the 2nd Battalion had just launched two groups of Landsers into the attack heavily supported by mortar teams. These troops corrected their aim until their shells burst right through the roofs of the buildings where the Russians were lying in wait. Where enemy fire persisted, the Landsers equipped with flame-throwers fixed to the muzzles of their 98K got rid of these last acts of resistance.

When the two groups of Landsers

The StuG III, the assault gun intended for supporting infantry units, was mounted on a Pz. III chassis and was also a formidable tank buster. Its low profile and its powerful 75-mm canon made it one of the German army's beasts of burden right up to the end of the conflict. Here the side armour has been reinforced by adding track links.

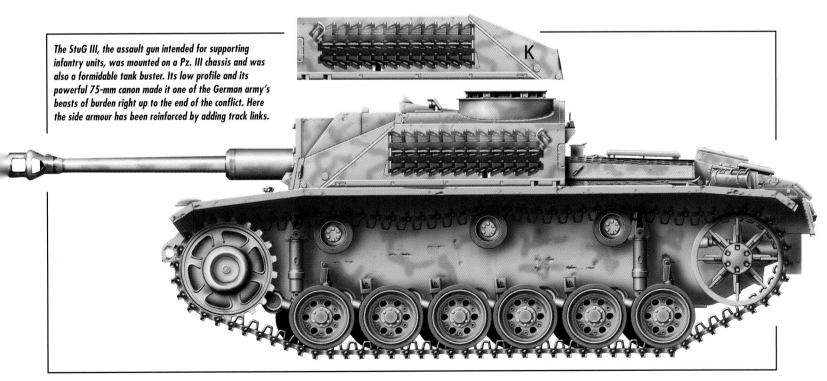

Above:
This OST-RSO Raupenschlepper, or tractor of the east, is probably towing a 75-mm or 6.62-cm anti-tank gun as it normally did. This tracked vehicle had been designed for use in Russia. It could carry three tonnes even across the most difficult terrain.
(BA 22/2925/06)

separated at a crossroads, one to head for the town centre, the other for the southern exit in order to join Major Vollmary's assault battalion, Russians suddenly appeared. Less than 200 yards separated the Red Army soldiers from the Germans, both ready to throw themselves at each others'throats. Suddenly two heavy machine guns opened up. They cut swathes through the Russians whilst other troops reacted by firing or throwing grenades.

The Grenadiere persevered stubbornly. They launched an attack, firing at point blank range at isolated infantrymen who resisted, then they bounded after the Russians, brandishing their bayonet or their sharpened spade.

Major Vollmary, one of the most reliable officers of the 168th headed with his men towards the centre of Staryzh Gorod which was on fire.

The Russians had quickly abandoned the town under fire from the Grenadiere.

Wearing a rubberised greatcoat, this Feldgendarme is directing traffic in the operations zone. Note the gorget. The Motorcyclist and the driver of the Raupenschlepper wait patiently for him to turn the green side of his signal in their direction. (BA 22/2925/17)

The Kdr. was not satisfied with this defeat. He asked the artillery to pick off the enemy as they fled. *"If Ivan comes back towards us, we'll look after him"*, the terrible Colonel commented.

With Staryzh Gorod occupied by two companies, Major Vollmary continued his attack in the Chutor sector. He succeeded in capturing the enemy positions with some difficulty. *"Some bunkers have been destroyed as have two machine gun positions"*, the unit's log recorded

Left:

This scene reminds one at once of the Sappers'fighting song: "We build roads through the fields and ruins, we attack on water through the fire of hell. We fight and we help, all of us always in the forefront, until the roads can be used for victory. Sappers to the front, these roads will make us free!" These enthusiastic, motivating lines in the barracks had a different echo out on the front. Most of the Sappers engaged on the Eastern front never returned home. They were always the first into the fray to open the way and always the last to leave, covering the other soldiers.
(BA 22/2925/15)

THE FIFTH DAY OF THE OFFENSIVE: 9 JULY 1943

Generalfeldmarschall von Manstein was well aware of the breach caused by III. Pz.Korps separating from II.SS-Pz.Korps which itself was continuing to advance and he asked Gen. d. Pz. Tr. Breith to get his 19. Pz.Div. to pivot towards the west. This move would thus surprise the Russians who were too busy trying to break the advance of the three Waffen-SS armoured divisions.

For Heersgruppe South, Operation Citadel now entered its second phase. Von Manstein and Watutin now got down to the real struggle.

Von Manstein knew that he could still hope for a favourable outcome since the Russian reserves on the Voronezh front were beginning to dwindle. He therefore staked everything on breaking the Russian defences in the very centre of the Voronezh front, at Proshorovka to be precise; this objective was allocated to II.SS-Pz.Korps.

But before sending this armoured corps alone in that direction, he protected its rear by launching an offensive using III. Pz.Korps. Von Manstein thus hoped that the respective wings of each of his armoured army corps would be able to close in on those Russian units which had managed to separate them by more than almost 20 miles. Moreover, he asked Breith to widen his front which he considered too narrow and too much out on a limb into enemy territory.

Gen. d. Pz. Tr. Breith decided not to go over to the offensive immediately and to wait until he had reduced the forces situated between Razumnoe and Severnizh.

With this in mind, he formed two tactical groups – Angriffsgruppe Nord and Angriffsgruppe Sud. The former, under von Hünersdorf, had to be ready in the sector between Melikhovo and Delnazhaya Yigumenka, and the latter under Generalleutnant Schmidt had to hold itself ready near Blishnaya Yigumenka.

ANGRIFFSGRUPPE NORD - 6. PZ.DIV.

General von Hünersdorf's mission was to reach the heights between Melikhovo and Delnazhaya Yigumenka (situated near the Donets), and then to push on in the direction of Shishino. The first stage was to get hold of Schlachovozhe. As a precaution he placed his 35 operational tanks from Panzergruppe Westoven - Pz.Rgt. 27 – in the north-western and western sectors of Melikhovo.

After remaining in the woods to the west of Melikhovo, the Panzers in Panzergruppe von Oppeln Bronikowski started to advance again. However the Russian observers spotted the supply trucks belonging to Staffel Müller meeting up with

the tanks from 6. and 8./Pz.Rgt. 11. They radioed the positions to the artillery batteries which did not waste any time getting the Panzers square in their sights, firing their shells and hitting several of them. Those that did not get hit tried to escape by moving around. The situation got worse when Russian anti-tank guns also started to have a go at them. It was right in the middle of this atmosphere of crisis and panic that the Panzerschützen met up Major Bäke. There were a great number of casualties.

Following this setback, Oberst von Oppeln Bronikowski decided to break off, leaving behind him an armoured section as rearguard under the command of Leutnant Arzbruster with two SPW companies from II./Pz.Gren.Rgt. 114. The remnants of the other companies headed for another wood where they re-organised.

Hill 230.5, located at less than _ mile from the Panzers led by a Leutnant from II./Pz.Rgt. 11 (Huchtmann or Arzbruster?), was too tempting a target for a young officer straight from tank school who was after promotion.

"Panzer Marsch!", he yelled to the tank commanders in his section. The Panzer-

fährer stepped on the pedals and went all out.

Under a deluge of fire thrown at them by the Russian artillery, the Panzerschützen trembled with fear and excitement as they got nearer the hill. They slipped forward with skill using the dips in the terrain for temporary cover. But Russian anti-tank guns, camouflaged and hidden a little further on, spat fire and steel at the Pz. IIIs and IVs which split up. Without thinking of themselves, Major Bäke's men rushed straight forwards without worrying about the anti-tank guns. The terrible flashes which spouted from the muzzles of their 75-mms conscientiously picked off and destroyed the enemy positions which had been set up on hill 230.5. It took Major Bäke's men only a few moments to conquer the heights.

This victory sparked off a reaction from the Russians: all of a sudden their front seemed to catch fire. Artillery pieces, anti-tank guns, Stalin's organs all went into action. The earth sprung up in showers; grass, trees and brushwood shrivelled up in the intense heat from the explosions and twirled around in the air. It was only a question of time before the Panzerschützen were victims of these shells.

"What can I do?" the young Leutnant asked his superior from inside his Pz. IV. All his crews had the feeling that they were condemned men, without hope. The explosions followed on each other at a hellish rate.

"There's only one thing to do; get yourself on the other side of the hill where the Russians can't see you and then wait until it all dies down," grumbled Major Bäke.

"As for the foxholes you left behind you when you attacked the hill, the infantry will clean them out."

Angriffsgruppe Nord continued its advance without encountering any opposition. It captured Delnazhaya Yigumenka in spite of determined resistance from a group of tanks, and then it continued its attack westwards from the station at Postnikov. The Russians launched tanks and infantry into the battle in order to stop these armoured elements which were fighting with such impressive firepower.

No counter-attack was in any way up to stopping Angriffsgruppe Nord's progress.

The situation of the armour in II./Pz.Rgt. 11 at the end of the day was as follows:	
Pz. II	5
Pz. III (lg)	17
Pz. III (K.)	5
Pz. IV	10
Pz. IV (Bef.)	2
Fl.Pz.	4
T-34	4

ANGRIFFSGRUPPE SUD - 19. PZ.DIV.

The second tactical group taken in hand by Generalleutnant Schmidt had to deal with the southern sector. He had get the Russians out of the town of Blishnaya Yigumenka once and for all, clear out the woods nearby of all enemy defences and then push on to Shishino.

Operations were placed under the command of Oberst von Bieberstein, Kdr. of Pz.Gren.Rgt. 114 which for the time being was still at Delnazhaya Yigumenka. He only had his first battalion and a few tanks from Panzergruppe von Oppeln Bronikowski at his disposal.

When his units moved up to the front, Oberst von Bieberstein reported to Generalmajor Schmidt that his scouts had spotted several Russian tanks dug in. Their cannon were pointing at the northern exit out of Delnazhaya Yigumenka. The area between the anti-tank ditch and the village was littered with mines which the Sappers could not remove because there was no cover. The sector was now dangerously invested by the Russians who had been reinforced since the previous evening's attack on Belogo Kolodeszha. Some troops had headed east shortly afterwards. According to radio surveillance, the German observers understood that the Russians were soon going to reach Hill 211.1.

Oberst von Bieberstein told 19. Pz.Div.'s Kdr. that his armoured infantry companies could at best check the enemy's advance, but not repel it. During the morning, Hauptmann von Kageneck, Kdr. of s. Pz.Abt. 503 learnt that he was to reinforce Kampfgruppe von Bieberstein. Once he got the message, he leapt into his Kübelwagen with his driver and went to Delnazhaya Yigumenka. The weather was very trying and the temperature was increasing. An hour and a half later, the Tiger captain managed to reach Generalleutnant Schmidt's command post, set up in a kolkhoz. Maps recovered from a T-34 were

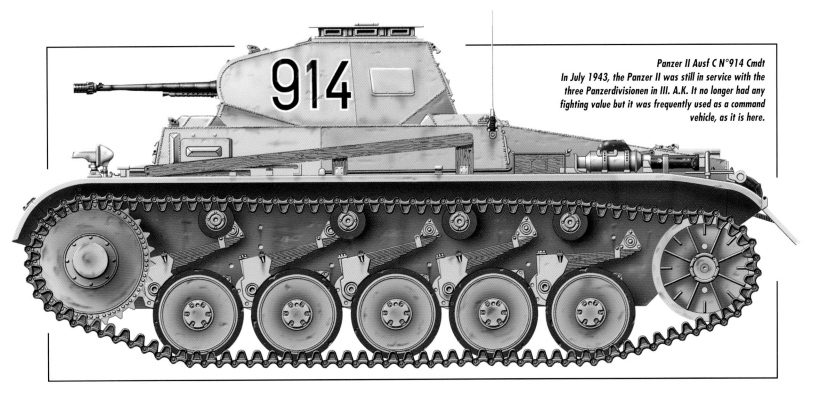

Panzer II Ausf C N°914 Cmdt
In July 1943, the Panzer II was still in service with the three Panzerdivisionen in III. A.K. It no longer had any fighting value but it was frequently used as a command vehicle, as it is here.

DOCUMENTARY REPORT WITH THE 6. PZ.DIV.

Above : *Still wearing his mackintosh, Generalmajor von Hünersdorf is examining a map with Oberst von Oppeln Bronowski. The latter had taken over command of Pz.Rgt.11 on 17 February 1943 and left it in October 1943 to take command of Pz.Rgt. 100 of 21. Pz.Div. Like Generalmajor von Hünersdorf, he was wounded on the afternoon of 13 July and hospitalised. During his convalescence he was awarded the German Gold Cross. He had been awarded the Knight's Cross on 1 January 1943.* (BA 22/2924/6)

Below:
Near the two senior officers from 6. Pz.Div., there are two command tanks from Pz.Rgt. 11. 914 was a Pz. III. The Sd Kfz 250/3 with its typical radio antenna belongs to Generalmajor von Hünersdorf who has already been seen in another report. (BA 22/2924/7)

Above:
Once the Kdr.'s directives have been transmitted, the divisional vehicles start off. Attempts are being made to maintain the momentum of III. Pz.Korps' offensive.
(BA 22/2924/14)

Top right :
On board the Sd Kfz 250/3 belonging to Generalmajor von Hünersdorf, the orders are transferred to the troops of 6. Pz.Div. (BA 22/2924/11)

Right:
The German motorised column has halted. One of its pieces (maybe two) has been destroyed as has the vehicle towing it. It was a 76.2-mm Pushka obr. 1939. This was a Russian anti-tank gun which had been issued only to 1./Pz.Jg.Abt. 41 from 6. Pz.Div. It had a range of 8 1/3 miles and a rate of fire of 25 shots a minute. The tactical insignia of 6. Pz.Div. can be seen on the front of the sidecar. A horse-drawn column is moving towards them, coming along a different route from the Panzerjäger.
(BA 22/2924/15)

Below:
The soldiers reach the entrance to a village. The rolls of barbed wire which surrounded it have been pushed aside by the assault troops. The officer wearing a forage cap, probably a company commander, is also wearing a camouflage tunic, like the group commander who is standing back slightly and who is armed with an MP40. One of the section commanders, walking next to the officer with a map in his hand, has found a PPSh 41 for himself. This sub-machine gun was in widespread use in the German army in Russia. This gun fired 500 rounds per minute thanks to its round magazines containing 71 rounds. One of these magazines can be seen here slipped through the NCO's belt and another one sticking out from behind his back next to the butt. The third soldier from the left is surely carrying a radio generator; this is suggested by the fact that he is wearing an antenna sheath on his belt as well as a black leather headphone case hanging on his right. (BA 22/2924/31)

Above:
After passing through a burning village, the Panzergrenadiere carry on their way on foot. An artillery tractor is overtaking them. The Panzergrenadier in the foreground is wearing a cotton camouflaged tunic. The two 6. Pz.Div. infantry divisions seem to have been issued with this item in large numbers. So the Gross Deutschland Division was therefore not the only unit to have been issued with this item. (BA 22/2924/27)

Below: *This Panzergrenadier who is having a rest has removed the left strap of his artilleryman's backpack on which he had attached the canvas of his tent. The way he is standing reveals the details of his flak jacket better. (BA 22/2924/33)*

These soldiers from 6. Pz.Div. are investing a village which has recently been subjected to an artillery barrage. The house on the right is still burning. The Russians have withdrawn but the barbed wire is still there. A handful of soldiers are pulling some of it away from the middle of the track.
(BA 22/2924/36)

A group of MG servers in turn enters the village. The first among them is carrying a round "snail" magazine for the MG 34 in his left hand. The man behind him is carrying an ammunition case for the machine gun. The strap hanging from this case is merely the carrying belt for the case which the infantryman clearly does not need to use.
(BA 22/2924/38)

Left:
Mechanics and crew of an Ilyushin B2 a short time before the Battle of Kursk. Informed of the German offensive, the Red Army Air Force intensified its attacks against German airfields and destroyed almost 250 machines.
(DR Caption by M. Chaubiron)

spread out on a table. Several officers were present.

19. Pz.Div.'s CO seemed to be very worried. And yet his high awards - Knight's Cross with Oak Leaves, German Gold Cross - and his long military career would seem to indicate that he had been through worse than this on the front.

Hauptmann von Kageneck just had time to salute "the Old Man" before he started giving out orders to his subordinates before they left for their combat positions.

"Bring me one of your companies immediately, Kageneck. It's got to be in place in an hour. Objective: Hill 211.1", thundered the General. *"A company of SPW will help you reach that hill. See Oberst von Bieberstein for the details."*

A short time later Oberst von Bieberstein's Panzergrenadiere saw several Tigers approaching with a deafening rumbling of engines. They were the last remaining tanks in 1./s. Pz.Abt. 503. The previous day, their CO could only scrape together four of them.

Hauptmann Burmester reviewed the situation with his Kommandeur then engaged his Tigers, passing behind a long hillock which protected the Russians. These Tigers were the vanguard of Angriffsgruppe Nord. Not finding any established positions, they progressed fairly quickly, at the same time staying in contact with the SPW companies who were holding back on their flanks.

Presently the Tigers reached the main front. Burmester suddenly issued a message to all his commanders. *"Watch out for anti-tank defences. Head straight for your objective!"* The Tigers attacked the hill using the most practicable flank and managed to open up a breach in the Russian disposition. After a few direct hits

from the 88-mms and a few bursts from the on-board machine guns, one Russian company was reduced to a couple of dozen men. The survivors were scared stiff of the powerful 58-tonne monsters. It was barely midday when Hauptmann Burmester announced that Hill 211.1 was theirs. This victory reassured Generalleutant Schmidt's headquarters. The situation however was not very enviable for Gren. Rgt. 442's and at any moment this risked putting the division in danger.

Although they were holding Blishnaya

Obergefreiter Fritz Bachmann had already served with 4.Pz.Div. and with the 320. I.D. before being transferred to 7. Pz.Div.
Formerly a first machine gunner, he became the division's foremost sharpshooter while in 1./Pz.Gren.Rgt.7. His unerring eye earned him a great reputation among his comrades. He showed extreme bravery in January 1945 during a counter-attack led by 7. Pz.Div. Generalleutnant Dr. Mauss put him up for the Ritterkreuz which he was awarded on 5 April 1945. He survived the war.
(Photo J. Charita. Coll. D.L.)

Yigumenka very firmly, the Grenadiers in this regiment from 168. I.D. were constantly under attack although they did manage to repel the enemy each time. Faced with such determined resistance, the Russians had got together some reinforcements during the night and since their arrival, the German infantry was slowly giving way under the weight of numbers.

Towards 12 o'clock, the Kdr. of Gren. Rgt. 442 was obliged to abandon part of the town. The regiment was reduced to a series of individual groups fighting mainly under the command of NCOs who had replaced their officers, wounded or killed in combat. There were a lot of casualties who would have to be cared for, but there were no doctors with them, only a few medics with no medical equipment or stretchers.

A despatch from 19. Pz.Div. HQ reached III. Pz.Korps. It contained these significant words: *"Gren. Rgt. 442 can no longer hold."*

There wasn't a moment was to lose. Generalleutnant Schmidt decided to take the initiative. He sent all his forces towards the forest situated to the south of Andreyevski where there was a large Russian defensive perimeter. Two groups from Art.Rgt. 248 (168. I.D.) were there to back them up.

In the night of 8-9 July 1943, two Russian infantry companies attacked Staryzh Gorod which was still in the hands of Major Vollmary. He outnumbered the enemy and got the better of them. Gren. Rgt. 429 held onto its positions without weakening.

The Scouts from Pz. AA 19 and the Panzergrenadiere from Pz.Gren.Rgt. 73 took two long hours to reduce the machine gun posts and the other positions with the help of the five tanks from 6. Pz.Div. Everybody was impressed by these Pz. IIIs equipped with flamethrowers on the turrets and built specially for close-quarter combat. When the Germans counted the dead at the end, they noted that not many Russians had survived.

Hauptmann von Kageneck also took part. According to a perfectly conceived plan, his Tigers attacked the enemy positions from the northeast. These were very quickly encircled. As soon as the attack was launched, 19. Pz.Div. and Kampfgruppe von Bieberstein succeeded in destroying three Russian tanks near Ovotsch. One of the armoured infantry officers, who had placed an observer on the fourth floor of a building ravaged by artillery fire, noticed that the Russians were moving to the north. He saw lots of columns of smoke rising in the direction of Shishino caused by the artillery pieces belonging to Oberst Proff who had taken on some Stalin's organs, destroying four of them.

The High Command of the Russian 7th Army, which had suffered heavy losses during the day, placed the 92nd Guards Division on the line facing Melikhovo - Blishnaya Yigumenka - Delnazhaya Yigumenka. There were a lot of casualties in 19. Pz.Div. for the 5-9 July 1943 period: 217 killed, 1 434 wounded and 77 missing, a total of 1 728 casualties. When it engaged its armoured regiment alongside the von Oppeln Bronikowski Panzergruppe it lost 23 tanks which left it with only 12.

THE 7. PZ.DIV. SECTOR

This division remained in position in order to head off the Russians who were advancing in the direction of Melikhovo. It repelled several attacks on the Solovzhev kolkhoz.

Pz.Gren.Rgt. 7 (from 7. Pz.Div.) was relieved by the I. and II. Battalions of Gren. Rgt. 326 (from 198. I.D.) between Batrazkazha Datscha and the huge forest situated to the south of Miassoyedovo. Their right flank was protected by elements from 106. I.D. The regiment's reserve consisted of III./Gren. Rgt.

The journey for these infantrymen started by train but they almost finished it on foot. All the troop transports belonging to III. Pz.Korps were in use and lorries were finally provided by KW. Transport Regiment 605 from the Army Corps. Unfortunately only Oberst Keiser's Gren. Rgt. 326 was able to reach the front.

The rest of the division with its horses waited to entrain. After they detrained south of Belgorod, the Landsers from Gren. Rgt. 326 had to get across the Donets even though this was under attack from the Russian Air Force. Several soldiers were killed before even being engaged. At two o'clock in the morning the exhausted Grenadiere were at last able to relieve the soldiers in Pz.Gren.Rgt. 7.

Two heavy groups from Art.Rgt.106 in 106.I.D., "lent" by XI.A.K., were en route to relieve 7. Pz.Div.'s artillery regiment.

Feldwebel Weigl with Tiger 324 scored an impressive tally of hits. On his black tunic, he is wearing the tank combat insignia and silver medal awarded to the wounded. The aluminium gunner's cord, apparently the 5th level and reserved for the tank units, is hanging from his right shoulder flap and is fixed to the first button on the tunic flap. (Photo: Weigl. Coll. D.L.)

Two others had just joined the 326th Grenadiere who were in need of support. Leutnant von Rosen, the veteran, evokes that day: "9 July started calmly enough. I had slept well as had many of the men. Pz.Rgt. 25 was covering the division's flank.

"There were no changes planned for today. I was ordered to go and see the Kdr. who asked me to reconnoitre the forest right at the end of a valley.

"During the night we heard the sound of tanks. Two of my Tigers remained on the heights to cover me. I drove my tank myself and Feldwebel Weigl who accompanied me, did likewise with his."

"The turret hatch was fastened down, the tank was ready for combat. Panzer Marsch! We followed along on the side of the slope over open ground to a point about 400 yards from the edge of a thick forest.

"We stopped to look. Nothing. We started off again when there was a flash. In a fraction of a second, a shot came straight at me followed by a second. A direct hit to the front. The air vibrated and I could not make anything out. I fired an explosive shell in what I supposed was the right direction. We were hit again several times, this time from the right. I drove our tank to the starting-off position. Both our Tigers were hit again superficially. But this time a sprocket wheel was damaged. The Russians knew that this was the Tiger's weak spot. My two Tigers which had stayed further back to cover us opened fire on the two elf-propelled guns which had appeared on the edge of the forest. The two of them cleared off quickly. I called up the Kdr. to report.

"In the evening, Feldwebel Grohmann appeared. His job was to note down everything that happened to the 3. Kp. I learnt that Oberleutnant Scherf was engaged with the company at Miassoyedovo. That was also where Gefreiter Schmidt fell, on 8 July.

"Grohmann also brought mail and parcels for the soldiers. A letter was always welcome. There was chocolate for everybody. I learnt that Leutnant Jammerath, my friend from the officer tank school at Wünsdorf had been killed on the first day of the attack.

"A letter from home! All's well, thank God!"

Right:
This exceptional picture shows 3./s. Pz.Abt. 503 moving through Kharkov for the 5 July offensive. Tiger 314 is in the foreground with Feldwebel Weigl up in the turret.
(Photo: Weigl. Coll. D.L.)

THE SIXTH DAY OF THE OPERATION CITADEL: 10 JULY 1943

Gen. d. Pz. Tr. Breith's forces, now facing due north had to bring their advance to a halt. They had been severely weakened by the fighting on the flanks of the army corps. Only 6. Pz.Div. still had some punch left in it, but it was under-strength and had to be reinforced.

In order to bring up extra firepower, the three Tiger companies were at last reunited, to the great satisfaction of Hauptmann Graf von Kageneck.

III. Pz.Korps now had to establish a solid base from which to carry out the definitive breakthrough, cutting the route that the Russian 5th Armoured Guards Army was taking to reinforce the 6th Guards Army.

168. I.D. was given the task of preparing the terrain. But to do this, the Kdr. had to bring back and assemble all the units which had been detached during the previous days, in particular its Gren. Rgt. 442 which was struggling to capture Blishnaya Yigumenka and which ought to have taken the road to Belgorod… the same could be said of the 2nd and 3rd Artillery groups. In order to support his Grenadiere to the north of Belgorod, Generalmajor de Beaulieu had

obtained air cover consisting of two Gruppen of Stukas.

THE 6. PZ.DIV. SECTOR

Under cover of night in a forest to the southwest of Melikhovo, Oberst von Oppeln Bronikowski reorganised his Abteilung into two simple companies. The first was assigned to Oberleutnant Spiekermann and the second to Oberleutnant Reutemann (who commanded 1./s. Pz.Abt. 503 in March 1944). The regiment still had 5 Panzer IIs, 17 Pz. IIIs (long), 5 Pz. IIIs (short), 10 Pz. IVs,

Left:
This Sd Kfz. 251/8 is equipped with a FuG5 antenna and its antenna structure. This ambulance half-track had a crew of three. It could transport six casualties: four sitting and two stretcher cases. It belonged to either the 1. or the 2. San. Kp. 57 of 6. Pz.Div. as indicated by the divisional insignia painted on the front of the vehicle. Above the armoured units' tactical insignia, there is the white cross which helped identify the medical units, as well as the letters SA painted on the left.
(© ECPAD DAT 1940- L10)

2 Befehlspanzers, three flamethrower tanks and 4 T-34s, in all 46 tanks.

As for the unit's other divisions, they were relieved by elements of 7. Pz.Div. in their former positions and they were now fighting in the Korotska sector hoping to head for Komintern.

6. Pz.Div. had to deal with several counter-attacks, especially the ones against Hill 203.3 where the Panzerjäger had relieved von Oppeln Bronikowski's Panzers. Even the T-34s could not break their resistance.

Panzergruppe von Oppeln Bronikowski and Kampfgruppe Unrein defended Melikhovo for several hours with the Russian artillery bombarding the town relentlessly; they did not manage to break the German's resistance however.

Towards the beginning of the afternoon, with a certain feeling of bitterness, the Russians came to the conclusion that their attacks were just not successful. A message received by radio ordered them to cease their attacks and to fall back and reinforce their lines of defence.

Closely following the way events were developing, Gen. d. Pz. Tr. Breith sent 6. Pz.Div. north in such a way as to enable 7. Pz.Div. to keep a hold on the right wing of III. Pz.Korps. Oberst Unrein was ordered to take Shliakovo with his Kampfgruppe (Pz.Gren.Rgt.4). The tanks in Panzergruppe von Oppeln Bronikowski would support him up to the crossroads situated a mile from Melikhovo; then they would set off in pursuit of any Russian elements fleeing in disorder. The Luftwaffe would cover both units.

But this was not a simple affair. The bad weather conditions made any flying operations impossible and a minefield placed near Melikhovo delayed Bronikowski's Panzers. Oberst Unrein's Panzergrenadiere however finally made it to the village where the Russians fought with even more determination

than before. The Germans were hounded relentlessly by Stalin's organs with their strident whistle. Taking no notice of this stubborn resistance, Oberst Unrein launched his men straight into an assault on the enemy positions. Several of them fell under fire. Shliakovo

Above: Two SPWs (Sd Kfz. 251 Auf A) from II./Pz.Gren.Rgt. 114, 6. Pz.Div.'s shock battalion under Hauptmann Necknauer. The Panzergrenadiere from this unit were at the forefront of the fighting during the whole battle. One of their greatest victories was the covering fire they gave the Sappers while they were building the bridge over the Rasumnaya. This success enabled them to consolidate a bridgehead beyond the river. (© ECPAD DAT1940 L9)

Right:
Vehicles of all sorts – the responsibility of 6. Pz.Div. – moving up to consolidate the bridgehead set up by von Oppeln Bronikowski's tactical group. The Steyr in the foreground belongs to 1./Pz.Jg.Abt. 41 which was equipped with Marders but also with tractor-drawn Pak 7.62-cms cannon. It seems to be towing an ammunition cart. The Feldwebel who is sitting over the door has hung up his powerful 10 x 50 binoculars. On the right, there is a Type L3000A Mercedes-Benz. The two Sd Kfz.s in the background are each towing an 88-mm Flak gun from the Heeres-Flakartillerie-Abt. (mot.) 298 (the 298th Anti-Aircraft Battalion of 6. Pz.Div.) This unit had eight of these guns and 29 20-mm Flak guns. Only one of the 88-mm Flak guns was lost between 5 and 18 July 1943. A Rauppenschlepper is approaching right in the background.
(© ECPAD DAT 1940- L13)

DOCUMENTARY REPORT FROM 3./S. PZ.ABT. 503

Above :
It's daybreak. The crews have a break after stopping their Tigers on the side of the track. Just like the Heer horseman, their attention is drawn to the wrecked truck, probably the victim of a Russian fighter. It is a Citroën Type 23 of 1939, more often called the U 23. The type was modified several times and several different versions saw the light of day after the war. This one came to end its days in the dust of a Ukrainian lane...
(BA 22/2935/9a)

Left:
Completely worn out, the Panzerschützen from Tiger 323 relax after spending part of the night driving and their uniforms are all creased. Two individual mess tins have been put on the front of the tank, near an ammunition box. Two of the three smoke canisters have been fired and the mudguard has been damaged. All these are signs that this Tiger has been engaged for several days now, if not several weeks.
(BA 22/2935/10a)

Left:
The Russian Air Force was very active in the area where III. Pz.Korps was engaged, so while waiting for new marching orders, the crew conceals its Tiger.
(BA 22/2935/18a)

Above:
Although the tank is now almost invisible, the same cannot be said of the tracks it has left behind it which have to be rubbed out, at least near where the machine is hidden. A Panzerschütze with a rake is therefore rubbing away all traces of the tank. Another man with a spade is trying to level out the ground. There must be no traces at all for enemy pilots to be able to locate the tank. These exhausting chores saved the crews' lives more than once.
BA 22/2935/19)

Top right:
The commander of Tiger 323, Unteroffizier Fütermeister shows the hits his tank received to Oberfeldwebel An Der Heiden, the CO of the 3rd section of 3. Kp. (BA 22/2935/25)

Middle right:
Oberfähnrich Rondorf, one of s. Pz.Abt. 503's aces talking to an army soldier. He kept wearing this double-breasted jacket during the whole of the summer 1943. Some of the Panzerschützen in s. Pz.Abt. 503 were still wearing this type of double-breasted jacket during the Battle of Normandy. (BA 22/2935/27a)

Right:
With their task completed the crew of Tiger 323 allow themselves a little rest behind their Tiger. There is the ammunition case already seen in the report. Note that the Panzerschützen stow their kitchen utensils (mess tins, cutlery, etc.) in a box. Some of them are taking advantage of this moment of calm to reread some letters from their loved ones. (BA 22/2935/32)

Left: *The fatigues jacket was ideal for the Panzerschützen in the hot season. This member of 323's crew has just received a letter which seems to have given him something to smile about.* (BA 22/2936/11)

letter from Obergefreiter Bleidiessel to his parents. 10 July 1943

"*My dear parents, Today my letter will be shorter than usual. The Russians are fighting with everything they've got in order to keep their positions. But they'll have to retreat. On the first day of the engagement we were hit by an anti-tank gun but nothing happened to the Tiger. Yesterday we ran over a mine but only the track was damaged. Tomorrow we'll be off again. The weather hasn't changed. It's cold, humid and rainy. Apart from that there isn't any news. We are engaged night and day. I'll write again soon...*"

Left: *After their break, the Panzerschützen have to get their shelter ready for the night. They have dug a large hole at the bottom of which they have piled up leaves for a mattress. The blankets are ready.* (BA 22/2936/13)

Left: *A Panzerschütze seems to be repairing one of the ventilator parts. This shot allows us to see how the number was painted on the turret.* (BA 22/2936/22)

could well have become the graveyard for Kampfgruppe Unrein, but for their Colonel's daring which paid off. The unit reached its objective.

Meanwhile, Panzergruppe von Oppeln Bronikowski, the spearhead of 6. Pz.Div., got through the mine field and moved north. The crews of Panzer 904 from the Stabskompanie had installed a new, very effective radio which enabled them to contact the Stukas (Fu G10).

THE 7. PZ.DIV. SECTOR

Starting the evening before and going on into the afternoon of 10 July, the Russians kept the pressure up on 7. Pz.Div.'s front. It was a little after 15.00 when the tractors brought up the last battery of Pz.Art.Rgt. 78 cannon. The regiment was now in its new position. Oberst Winkler kept on sweeping the forest with his binoculars: he knew it hid a large number of Russian units. For the moment, the enemy was not showing itself and this worried him. According to his orders, his guns opened fire at 16.00, firing into the forest facing their front line.

The Landsers in Gren. Rgt. 326 from 198.I.D. also took part in this assault by attacking the northern part of this forest where a huge concentration of mortar positions had been localised. As for the Panzers in Pz.Rgt. 25, they left their positions in order to engage the enemy over open terrain. Oberstleutnant Schulz quickly positioned his

Oberst Friederich Quentin and his Scouts carried out the reconnaissance missions for 6. Pz.Div. Commanding Pz. AA.6, he was awarded the Knight's Cross on 8 February 1943. Before that he was CO of II./Pz.Gren.Rgt. 114 which had earned him the German Gold Cross.
(Photo J. Charita. Coll. D.L.)

command tank behind a spinney where he could observe the progress of his tanks, now covered by Luftwaffe aircraft which dived on the forest dropping incendiary bombs. In turn, 7. Pz.Div.'s assault battalions joined the tanks to cover their flanks.

Within a few minutes, the forest developed into a huge bonfire. The bombing completely disorganised the Russians and their casualties were very heavy. The Panzergrenadiere cap-

tured the bunkers situated on the edge of the forest using their grenades and Schmeissers. The Russian infantry engaged in bloody fighting where there was no such thing as pity. It only took the Grenadiers of the 326th two hours to break the resistance of the Russian defenders. Although the Grenadiers destroyed a lot of enemy machine gun, mortar and anti-tank positions, the trap was closing in on them. Their right wing was threatened by a Russian attack in order. Likewise, the Russians crept up upon the village of Batrazkazha Datscha from the north.

Why was Gren. Rgt. 326 so cursed? Dazed, the Landsers were particularly courageous as they faced the repeated Russian assaults. In proportion to the enemy's greater numbers, their own losses were very heavy and the regiment's CO urgently called up the reserve battalion in order to try to balance out the forces, but it was not enough.

In the end it was the entire 198. I.D. under Generalmajor von Horn which intervened to shore up Gren. Rgt. 326 whose situation had become very shaky. Once the situation was restored and under control, the division's Kdr. was ordered to consolidate his positions and to hang on to them.

Ex-Leutnant von Rosen, who was probably situated to the north of this forest at the time, tells the story of that day:

"I'd been on duty since dawn. Suddenly the Russians left their positions, set up in a forest, and went away to set

This troop transport was in service with the Panzergrenadiere regiments, although there were not enough of them to equip all the companies. An MG 34 or 42 could be mounted on the anti-aircraft gun carriage at the rear of the hull.

up others elsewhere. I couldn't believe my eyes. One, two then three tanks appeared briefly and then disappeared at full speed behind a natural shelter. My pointer thought he was having hallucinations too.

"We opened fire. No direct hit. We corrected our aim. Fire, smoke, white fog which hid everything from sight. Calm returned. Suddenly a dozen tanks charged us. We got rid of one, perhaps even a second one.

"There was a lot of activity around the Panzers. We checked our weapons, then studied the maps spread out in the sun. How long was this calm going to last. We took advantage of it to gather strength. I went to HQ a couple of times. No news from the front. The Kdr. offered me a drink. Humanity was taking over again from war."

Schülz's Panzers left the forest to the Panzergrenadiere who started to clear it out. But what Pz.Rgt. 25's Kdr. did not know was that a Russian regiment heading for the southern part of the same forest was about to run into him. So for twenty-four hours, the infantry accompanying 7. Pz.Div. fought until

Below:
The Landsers from 168.I.D. do not cut a very fine figure with their Russian carts which they requisitioned for transport. All the Reich's effort in terms of equipment and weapons was predominantly concentrated in favour of the armoured divisions.
(© ECPAD DAT1940 L6)

reinforcements arrived.

Oberstleutnant Schülz pointed on the map to where the hills were situated, a mile to the north of Miassoyedovo. He ordered the Kdr. of II. Abteilung: "You're to get your tanks working again and get hold of those damned hills. Then the road for Miassoyedovo will be open and we can join up with our comrades in 6. Pz.Div."

Meanwhile a second infantry regiment from 198.I.D. arrived in turn to relieve other units in 7. Pz.Div.

THE 19. PZ.DIV. SECTOR

In order to support 168. I.D. when it attacked, the armoured division under Generalleutnant Schmidt had to concentrate its troops on its left wing so as to be able to attack the 81st Guards Infantry Division. The town and the region around Blishnaya Yigumenka were the backbone of the enemy forces' disposition.

During the night, Major Horst was ordered to gather together the remnants of Pz.Gren.Rgt.73 and then to fight alongside Major Wilmsen's Scouts. The Landsers from Gren. Rgt. 224 continued fighting. Kg. 73 swept aside the Russian positions two miles north of the town, taking prisoners and routing the enemy who abandoned part of their equipment.

Small groups of Grenadiers managed

to infiltrate into the built-up area, defending houses they had taken with their sub-machine guns or their 98Ks. The town seemed to vanish in the smoke of the explosions. Gradually, the Germans succeeded in cutting the telephone lines and isolating in turn groups of Russians who fell to the heavy mortar shells.

After taking Blishnaya Yigumenka Gren. Rgt. 442 was reattached to its division and was ordered to position itself on the right flank. A lot of Russian infantrymen scurried from their positions to try and escape from the Grenadiers who were combing the town.

At midday, two Flak Abteilungen deployed their AA batteries which they pointed to the north of Delnazhaya Yigumenka. Their comrades in the Artillery copied them. Then towards one p.m., all hell was let loose on that particular zone marked out by Generalleutnant Schmidt. Once the terrain was cleared, his units got together and reorganised themselves.

Major Wilmsen's Scouts – Pz.A.A.19 – went out reconnoitring throughout the day. Some groups even managed to get deep behind the Russian lines in order to bring back vital information for the following operations. The Generalleutnant Schmidt's Stab thus learnt on one hand that Kisselovo and Shatchovo were very strongly defended by the Russians. On the other hand they also learnt that the Scouts had spotted a very big west-east

troop movement together with troops moving to the south of Hill 211.5, and to Shpaki. During this reconnaissance, Major Wilmsen's Scouts had noticed British tanks, Churchills, and had taken the opportunity to destroy two of them.

Meanwhile, Kampfgruppe von Bieberstein was locked in a merciless struggle on a line from Postnikov Station and Andreyevski. After three separate assaults, his men took the Russian positions. Once he was master of the field,

Oberst von Bieberstein ordered his men to get hold of Glavplodoavitch, a village situated to the south of Shishino.

The Scouts from Pz. AA 6 under Major Quentin surrounded the woods situated a mile to the north of Andreyevski during the night of 9-10 July. Finally, in the grey light of dawn, 6. Pz.Div.'s reconnaissance battalion's vehicles fell upon their target.

Driving their vehicles in a swirl around the woods, firing machine gun bursts

into the trees, they encircled the Russians who could do nothing but send out a cry for help to the command post while the pressure from the Scouts continued to increase.

Major Quentin decided to launch his

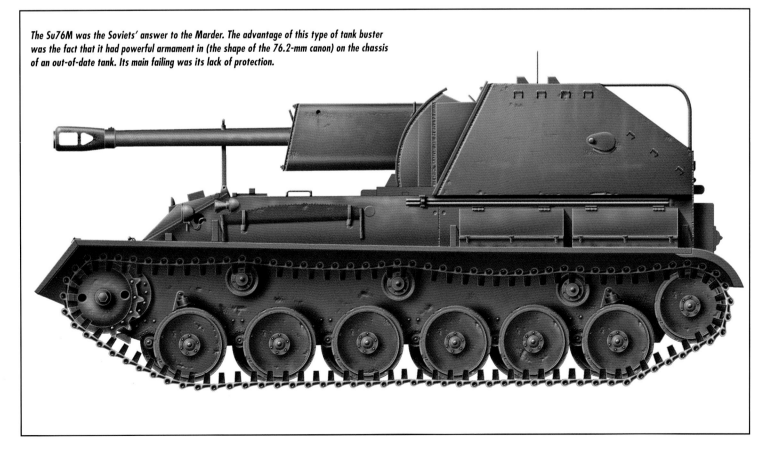

The Su76M was the Soviets' answer to the Marder. The advantage of this type of tank buster was the fact that it had powerful armament in (the shape of the 76.2-mm canon) on the chassis of an out-of-date tank. Its main failing was its lack of protection.

Above:

This infantry canon is a 75-mm leichtes Infantriegeschütz 18. There were two versions, one for motorised units with rubber tyres, and another for horse-drawn units with metal-rimmed wooden wheels like in this photograph. It could fire between eight to twelve rounds a minute and had a range of two and a quarter miles with a normal charge and nearly three miles with a more powerful charge. It had been in production since 1927 and served until the end of the war. (BA 219/594/33)

men at Kalinina and capture it. They only got hold of part of the town because they came across determined resistance in the northwest suburbs. Quentin therefore left one company from his battalion to hold the town and sent the others to clean out the woods situated to the southwest of Kalinina, as well as the Schipoffau Kalinina school sector.

Suddenly the Scouts spotted a large movement of Russian troops: they were approaching the western part of the town. For Major Quentin there was never any question of recalling his companies if they were engaged elsewhere. He had no choice but to warn Divisional HQ and ask them to get him out of his predicament.

A short while afterwards, the Panzergrenadiere from II./Pz.Gren.Rgt. 114 jumped into the regiment's half-tracks. Their Kdr., Hauptmann Necknauer, was afraid they could run out of ammunition but there was no time to waste, they were in a hurry. He launched the attack in record time with the support of three Tigers from s. Pz.Abt. 503. His SPW reached the road west of the town, and then with a quick turning movement, they rushed the Russians

who were getting ready to make a frontal counter-attack on the town! The Russians were taken by surprise by Necknauer's battalion who attacked them on their flank. The 88-mm barrels barked. In a confused but brief fight, the Russians were beaten by the unending fire kept up by the Germans and the noose started very quickly to tighten around them.

INITIATIVES FOR 168. I.D.

The attack which 168.I.D. had planned to the north of Belgorod could only be carried out in perfect coordination with 167.I.D. which was situated to the west of the Donets, therefore in the II.SS-Pz.Korps sector. There was only the river to separate these two infantry divisions whose mission was identical: cover the armoured divisions' rear. This far from glorious role is the main reason why History only remembers the action of the Panzerdivisionen and not the others.

First, the attention of the 168.I.D. observers was drawn to the departure of the Russian 375th Infantry Division, whose forces were spread out along the

line to the west of Shopino – Temovka – Visloya. Scout patrols were sent to see what was going on and keep an eye on this unexpected movement.

To the west of the Donets, General-major von Hütner of the 167.I.D. was worried when he saw these enemy units crossing the river and heading in the direction of his Gren. Rgt. 331. Shortly afterwards, he learnt from a group of Scouts from Gren. Rgt. 315 that the enemy units were setting up a line of defence between Hill 192.6 – Visloya and the edge of the forest situated to the north of the Promovya ravine.

In the early light of day, formations of Russian bombers first attacked 167.I.D.'s positions, then 168.I.D.'s. The artillery-men took their revenge by sending to the scrap yard six tractor-drawn cannon which were moving southwards.

At 7 o'clock, the Russians broke through the heart of the 168.I.D. Landsers' frontline under a deluge of mortar, heavy and light artillery shells and Katyusha rockets.

Generalmajor von Hütner ordered his division over to the attack. If his troops could break the resistance of the Russians to the west of the Donets, the flank of the 375th Guards Infantry Division would be under threat and its frontline which was already under attack by 168.I.D. would run the risk of collapsing everywhere. As a result, the salient which had been separating II.SS-Pz.Korps from III. Pz.Korps since the very beginning of the offensive would disappear and this would lead to the 89th and 92nd Guards Infantry Divisions having to fall back. It was worth taking the risk.

Despite terrible artillery and Katyusha fire and although deprived of one of their infantry regiment busy relieving the Das Reich units, 167.I.D.'s infantry nevertheless attacked early in the morning.

By some sort of miracle, Gren. Rgt. 331 occupied Shopino and II./Gren. Rgt. 315 broke through into the region situated to the west of Visloya Soshankov

Oberleutnant Günter Hasenbeck was in good hands with his Kdr., Major Quentin of Pz. AA.6, who gave him command of one of his companies. The Knight's Cross was already hanging from his collar before Kursk. He had been awarded it on 13 May 1943.
(Photo J. Charita. Coll. D.L.)

under the same conditions. 168.I.D. joined up with 167.I.D. at Shopino. This

threatened the soldiers in the 375th Guards Infantry Division, who had to reinforce their positions to the west of the Donets. They held on to the bridge which had enabled them to cross the Donets to attack 167.I.D. All the groups of Scouts that had infiltrated their zone were very quickly localised and submitted to intense gunfire. If they remained where they were they would be massacred. Giving up their observation posts, they fell back rapidly and rejoined their lines. Generalmajor von Hütner did not get the information he needed to plan his operation to the east of the Donets.

Throughout its various engagements, 168.I.D. captured about 300 prisoners and a lot of weapons, as borne out by these figures: 96 light machine guns, 14 heavy machine guns, 71 rocket-launchers, 21 heavy mortars, 20 light mortars and eight anti-tank guns.

When darkness enveloped the northwest of Belgorod, wisps of black smoke from the burning wrecks of 170 Russian tanks could be seen drifting upwards from miles away. After five days' fighting, the starting base for the breakthrough Generalfeldmarschall von Manstein had been after was established.

The horse-drawn artillery companies were made up of four sections of two guns, eight in all. Each canon was drawn by horse-drawn limber. As seen here, there were six 75-mm Infanteriegeschütz servers. Apart from its cannon, each section was equipped with 27 Mauser 98Ks and nine pistols. (BA 219/594/34)

THE SEVENTH DAY OF THE OFFENSIVE: 11 JULY 1943

Generalfeldmarschall von Manstein understood that victory for the Army Group South depended on Gen. d. Pz. Tr. Breith of III. Pz.Korps and that was why he came to visit him at the armoured corps HQ. The "strategist" asked Breith for a detailed report on the state and strength of his three armoured divisions. Their make-up would determine events in the near future.

Although Pz.Rgt. 27 (19. Pz.Div.) was but a shadow of its former self, two armoured regiments of 6. and 7. Pz.Div. (Pz.Rgt. 11 and 25) were still strong enough to be able to envisage a bold operation.

Indeed, Generalfeldmarschall von Manstein wanted to neutralise some of the Russian forces on Watutin's Voronezh front so that he could get hold of Proshorovka, the last important town before reaching Kursk.

III. Pz.Korps still had 116 Panzers of all types. This was a surprising figure considering the severe fighting which had raged during the last six days. This exploit was not only due to the Kdrs. of the armoured Abteilungen but also to the repair workshops who worked day and night.

Victory seemed close but nothing was won yet because Watutin still had a few

cards up his sleeve. His 69th Army and his 2nd Guards Corps had been able to block III. Pz.Korps. As for his 2nd Guards Armoured Corps, it could dislocate the German attack by breaking both the right wing of II.SS-Pz.Korps and the left wing of III. Pz.Korps. A river however protected the wing which both these army corps had in common.

Generalfeldmarschall von Manstein asked Gen. d. Pz. Tr. Breith to gather together his two armoured divisions and launch them in the direction of the Russian 69th Army with the aim of driving it back at all costs. II.SS-Pz.Korps had to have room to manoeuvre in order to wrest Proshorovka from the 5th Guards Army. If the two armoured divisions succeeded, they could get round this Russian army, isolating the 69th Guards Army on its east flank and thus cutting it off from

the 6th Guards Army through the intervention of II.SS-Pz.Korps.

Generalfeldmarschall von Manstein's plan turned out to be excellent but there was still the threat posed by the 7th Guards Army: it still had fresh divisions situated all along the front with XI.A.K., in the Koren sector and these were capable of attacking in force on the eastern

Top:
This Landser is examining a T-34/76 which has burnt out, as shown by the missing rubber bands on the wheels and the piles of ashes where they should have been. Note the tree trunk on the right side mudguard and the handles on the turret for the infantry who often rode on the engine cowling because of the severe lack of transport. This is one of the 1 600 Russian tanks (or assault guns) destroyed during Operation Citadel. As for the German armoured troops fighting in the Orel, Kursk and Karkhov areas, they lost 1 331 tanks between 5 July and 31 August 1943.
(BA 219/553/36)

92

flank of III. Pz.Korps when it moved north-wards.

THE 6. PZ.DIV. SECTOR

Generalmajor von Hünersdorf still had 40 Type III and IV tanks from II./Pz.Rgt. 11 at his disposal and he ordered them to assemble quickly with a view to launching the assault on Olkhovatka.

To Hauptmann von Kageneck's great satisfaction, the three Tiger companies in s. Pz.Abt. 503 were working together on this operation. A week had passed however and now there were only 19 Tigers left fit for battle.

According to his orders, Leutnant von Rosen had to join up with the 3. Kp. early in the morning. "I designated the meeting point on the map which was only a few miles from our position. My attachment to Pz.Rgt. 25 was drawing to an end. I told my Kdr. who said to me 'Well done, good work! We did a good job together'. In order to find 3.Kp., I had to pass through Miassoyedovo which was still not entirely safe. I decided to take the shortest route.

"As soon as we started crossing no man's land, I ordered my men to action stations. The turret hatches were closed. All was well for the moment but I knew it would not last for long.

"Behind a winding track, I glanced at the immense field which we were about to cross. RRRRMMMMSSS. Fire! The tank was in darkness, the lights weren't working any more. My right hand was stuck violently between the turret hatch cover and the breach. "Shit!" Unteroffizier Ziegler, the driver, got to the back of the tank. In only a few seconds all reactions became automatic again. The Tiger fired

an explosive shell which annihilated an anti-tank gun in the middle of the track, only thirty yards away. What had happened?

"We'd blindly driven over a shell the same calibre as ours. It did not get through the armour but it did cause a sever shock. The Tiger's 88-mm had jumped off from its crown and the muzzle break was no longer in alignment. In dropping down, the long tube caused the breach to swing upwards into the turret hatch cover.

"Fortunately, we were able to put the sights back in place and the canon was operational again and I was thus able to get myself out. My wound was bleeding a lot. The pointer, Unteroffizier Fütermeister gave me first aid, and I returned to my post as Commander, although I was still a bit stunned. We set off. I ordered another tank however to take over the section's pointing for me. Once again my guardian angel had been

Above:

Tiger 300 had to be abandoned by its crew because the towing team had not been able to get to them in time. Unteroffizier Jaeckel remembers that he replaced the pointer, Erwin Glas, who had been killed on 11 July, and that the track runners had been damaged a few days later. On top of that a shell had slightly displaced the mantlet, which had queered the barrel. The crew had had to wait for the arrival of the towing section but they had been forced to abandon the tank under pressure from the Russians. The holes to the front were made after the Tiger was abandoned. (Photo: D.R.)

around at the right time. We went along now with the hatch open.

"There were no other incidents. A huge rocket shot up into the sky in front of us. It was a signal from our group. We answered in the same way. We approached a vehicle from Pz. AA 7 which was on guard. It was all over. Another quarter of an hour and we reached the meeting point. I made out a report to Oberleutnant Scherf and the Abteilung's doctor looked after my wound. He cut through the right sleeve of my

In 1943, the T-34 revealed itself to be more manoeuvrable than a lot of light tanks. The thickness of its frontal armour was very much the same as that of the Tiger.

DOCUMENTARY REPORT WITH THE S. PZ.ABT. 503

by Bild Berichter Wolf-Allvater from P.K. 637
(637th Propaganda Company) (ECPAD DAT 3015)

Above: *Sitting in the Panzerführer's seat, Leutnant Weinert and Oberleutnant Scherf talking quietly during a break for a smoke.* (ECPAD DAT 3015- L7)

Right:
Oberleutnant Scherf designating a point on the map to a subordinate, an NCO most likely, given the stripe sewn round the collar. He has tucked the bottom of his combat jacket inside his trousers. This was common practice among the Panzerschützen. (© ECPAD DAT 3015 L10))

Middle right: *A Funker (radio operator) resting and listening to the news from home.* (© ECPAD DAT 3015 - L9)

Below left:
A Supply Corps team has stopped their kitchen lorry to which a trailer has been hitched. Some of them are busy camouflaging the vehicle while others watch them, just waiting for dinner. One of them is filling water cans from Kanisters. On the right the HQ liaison officer has also stopped to talk with friends in the kitchens and among the Panzerschützen. His partner has climbed down from his motorbike. (© ECPAD DAT 3015- L11)

Below right:
A briefing by Hauptmann Burmester (map in hand). Some of the 503rd's main characters are present: Hauptfeldwebel Haase (1st on the left), Oberfähnrich Rondorf (jodhpurs and camouflaged jacket), Oberfeldwebel Burgis (in shirt sleeves and braces). (© ECPAD DAT 3015- L24)

Tiger 300 seen from another angle. This shot most certainly comes from Russia and was taken in a place where other Tigers from s. Pz.Abt. 503 had been assembled before being photographed. (Photo: D.R.)

camouflaged tunic and revealed a huge cut in my flesh, from the bone to the elbow. The following day I was sent to the hospital in Kharkov. For me Operation Citadel was over. I was happy that there were no dead in my section."

Suddenly it started to rain so heavily that it prevented the units from joining up at Melikhovo on time. As a result Gen. d. Pz. Tr. Breith changed the time of the attack.

Having left for Olkhovatka three hours earlier, s. Pz.Abt. 503's 19 Tigers managed to reach the tanks belonging to 7. And 8./Pz.Rgt. 11. Now they had to open a way for them.

Growling engines broke the oppressive quiet of the night and the tank tracks churned up the water soaked earth as they moved. It was only after crossing the Delnazhaya Yigumenka – Schlachovozhe road that the Tigers and the Panzers from Pz.Rgt. 11 came under fire from the Russian anti-tank guns and artillery. The observers had spotted them. The Panzers returned the fire and got away quite easily and carried on advancing further through the Russian defences without being worried until the Russian artillery reacted and started aiming at them.

It was then that Oberst von Oppeln

Bronikowski proposed a plan of attack: the armoured group would split into two forces: the 8./Pz.Rgt.11 group would assault one of the heights where the artillery was located.

The second made up of s. Pz.Abt. 503 and 7. Pz.Div. would continue towards its objective: Olkhovatka.

The plan would have probably broken down when 8./Pz.Rgt. 11's armour met a wide minefield had they not made a relatively easy manoeuvre and gone round this field successfully. As a result it only slowed them down a bit and they continued on their way without loss.

The Russian armour now tried to break

Tiger 300 belonging to Oberleutnant Scherf. After being damaged, it could not be repaired and had to be abandoned. The driver of this tank was Unteroffizier Gotthold Wünderlich.

the Panzers' advance by firing from Hills 220 and 230.3. Panzer 904 belonging to Leutnant Knust received a direct hit. He recalls: *"Nish, Rayer and Morisse were wounded and the Stukaleitgerät (Stuka radio set) could not be used during the attack."* But the 8./Pz.Rgt. 11 tanks succeeded in slipping away to Hill 230.3.

The other tanks got into Olkhovatka where they created disorder and panic. A short time later Oberleutnant Spiekermann slipped into a wood for a short rest and then set off boldly north-eastwards to get to Schlachovozhe.

In order also to reach this village, the 7./Pz.Rgt. 11 tanks forced a breach almost two miles wide through the Russian 305th Division's lines. However, the strongpoint that had been set up at Schlachovozhe was only taken after a very hard fight.

Encouraged by this success and under Major Bäke's watchful eye, the 7. Kp. continued to advance into enemy territory, sweeping aside all resistance on its way. It was soon joined by the s. Pz.Abt. 503 Tigers. It was not long before this armoured group was greeted by salvoes from the Russian artillery; but these did not even slow its advance down. It soon came into sight of Olkhovatka.

To Major Bäke's surprise, capturing the village was a relatively easy affair without any opposition worth mentioning. On the other hand the Panzerkampfgruppe's advance towards Snamenka turned out to be much more difficult since there were resistance points which had been expertly set up, especially when the Germans started to approach Hill 223.3, where a hail of Katyusha rockets were fired down at them from.

Oberst von Oppeln Bronikowski was careful to avoid a confrontation which he considered to be useless. He launched his tanks towards Snamenka which they captured easily. He next headed east for about a mile and a half before turning towards the small town of Verkhni Olshanetz, a town which was the last lynchpin before Kasatzh and a much more important objective than Hill 223.3 because it was situated due north.

Worry clouded the face of Hauptmann Graf von Kageneck when he saw the Russian defences set up in front of Verkhni Olshanetz. They seemed to extend to the southeast as far as the eye could see.

The Tiger Kdr. was right to be worried: he had just come across the lines of another enemy division: the 107th Infantry Division. He has given us a singularly realistic description of the Russian defences.

"Every day we had to break through defensive barriers including anti-tank

Im Namen des Führers und Obersten Befehlshabers der Wehrmacht

verleihe ich

dem

Leutnant von R o s e n, 3./Pz.Abt. 503,

das

Eiserne Kreuz 1. Klasse

.Div.Gef.Stand...,den..23..Juli....19.43 /

Generalmajor u.Div.-Kommandeur

(Dienstgrad und Dienststellung)

positions on both flanks. Once, when I was on one of the hills with my Tiger, I could make out down below me a trench full of Russian soldiers wearing their brown uniforms rapidly handing out Molotov cocktails. As our machine gun was in a blind spot, there was only one way out, step on it and get out!"

7./Pz.Rgt. 11 took the village which in the end was weakly defended. Meanwhile, the other Panzers pushed on east, in the direction of Kasatzh, a town heavily defended by Russian tanks which had taken the trouble to dig themselves in up to the turret.

The mission of freeing this enclave and taking the town at the same time fell to Pz.Gren.Rgt.4 which carried it out with efficiency. Towards 10 p.m., it was joined by Panzergruppe von Oppeln Bronikowski which was getting ready to settle down. But the crews did not have the opportunity: von Manstein entrusted them with another mission, a suicide mission which had to be carried out during the night.

THE 7. PZ.DIV. AND 19. PZ.DIV. SECTORS

The role of these two divisions was restricted to protecting 6. Pz.Div. thus enabling it to play a major role.

Some diversionary operations fell to 19. Pz.Div. It had to take Krivtsevo and Strelnikov in order to lure away the Russian 81st and 89th Divisions situated to the west of the Donets. Moving these two divisions would take the pressure off 6. Pz.Div. on its western flank and enable it to reach its objectives during the day.

To make 19. Pz.Div. operational (it was not strong enough to protect 6. Pz.Div.), Gren. Rgt. 429 from 168.I.D. was attached to it.

This infantry regiment's task was to advance in unison with 19. Pz.Div. moving along the eastern bank of the Donets; it would thus prevent the Russian forces situated on the western bank of the river from doing anything in the sector of Generalleutnant Schmidt's armoured division.

As for Generalmajor von Funck's 7. Pz.Div., it protected III. Pz.Korps' eastern flank, blocking the Russians and preventing them from isolating 6. Pz.Div. It got itself reorganised during the early hours of the day then re-stocked with ammunition, fuel and general supplies for the day.

198.I.D.

Placed on the eastern flank of III. Pz.Korps, 198.I.D. protected the rear of the three armoured divisions and 168.I.D.

Its three infantry regiments were in the line before daybreak.

One of them, Gren. Rgt. 326, had been in place since the previous day and relieved part of 7. Pz.Div.'s front. Its I./Gren. Rgt. 326 occupied the Batrazkazha Datscha kolkhoz, a strongpoint in the German line of defence; the Russians had been trying very hard to get hold of this stronghold, attack after attack since 7 a.m. Enemy artillery tried to blast this cooperative out of existence, but the building's walls and the concrete shelter were so thick that they resisted even the heaviest-calibre shells. It was only late in the evening that the battalion fell back into the zone of III./Gren. Rgt. 326 (under Oberstleutnant Zimmermann) which was still placed in reserve.

Shortly afterwards, both battalions were ordered to *"clarify"* the situation at Batrazkazha Datscha.

Leutnant Munz's heavy company (10./Gren. Rgt. 326) supported the Grenadiere who were quite determined to encircle the town.

One of the company commanders, Oberleutnant Ackermann, volunteered to go out reconnoitring with some Landsers. But the Batrazkazha Datscha defenders spotted them and the mortars were not slow in reacting. The brave company commander was hit by shrapnel in the head and killed. For their baptism of fire, the Grenadiere behaved just like old veterans of the front. They tightened the noose round the town then cleared out each sector, one by one. Capturing the town enabled the Kdr. of the I. Btl. to take up

his quarters in the kolkhoz sector again.

At 12.20, near Batrazkazha Datscha, I./Gren. Rgt. 326 was attacked by surprise by a Russian battalion supported by sustained heavy mortar fire. After an hour's fighting and with the support of the infantry, the Grenadiere managed to break the enemy attack.

This time the Russians seemed to be discouraged by the unremitting resistance this infantry regiment put up. So in the end, they were content to harass the German unit from time to time, for the

Above:
A typical Soviet propaganda photograph. In the Red Army there were no war correspondents as there were in the German army. Many of the shots were taken after the war during "reconstitutions".
(DR Caption by M. Chaubiron)

rest of the afternoon. Artillery, mortar and machine gun exchanges were frequent.

As the front was relatively calm, the Sappers from Pi.Btl. 235 laid hundreds of anti-tank mines along a forest road where the Russian tanks were expected

T-34 1943-model. In reply to the heavy losses suffered by the T-34s in Battle of Kursk, the Soviets gave it an 85-mm canon which was much better suited to long-range duels with German tanks.

DOCUMENTARY REPORT FROM 198.I.D.

Above:
This scene illustrates an infantry unit moving up into the line during the Battle o[f] Kursk. It could be 198.I.D. As of 9 July 1943, Gren. Rgt. 326 (from 198.I.D.) was attached to 7. Pz.Div. But the unending attacks by the Russians who drew on forces that outnumbered the Germans, obliged XI A.K. to send the whole of 198.I.D. into 7. Pz.Div.'s zone. (BA 198/1384/7)

Left: At dawn of 11 July, it was the Landsers from Gren. Rgt. 305 together with two companies from Pi.Btl.235, who arrived near Generalovka, a sector attributed to 7. Pz.Div. They assembled in the woods situated a mile to the eas[t] of the town. A third infantry regiment from 198.I.D., Gren. Rgt.308, moved up into the line at the beginning of the morning. (BA 198/1384/9)

Organogramme

Kdr. : Generalleutnant Hans-Joachim von Horn

Grenadier-Regiment 305 :	Oberstleutnant Grassmann
I./Gren. Rgt. 305 :	Hauptmann Thierfelder
Grenadier-regiment 308 :	Oberst Schultz
Grenadier-Regiment 326 :	Oberst Keiser
III. Btl. -	Oberstleutnant Zimmermann

Füsilier-Bataillon 198
Artillerie-Regiment 235
Pionier-Bataillon 235
Panzerjäger-Bataillon 235
Nachrichten-Abteilung 235

Left: The infantry carrying on their advance under the watchful eye of an Oberleutnant, probably their company commander, who has earned the German Gold Cross. Two of them are carrying the heavy tube of an 8.1-cm mortar. Each of the three sections of an infantry company was equipped with one of these Granatwerfers (Grenade thrower) as it was called in the German Army. Apart from this heavy weapon, each section also had 33 Mauser 98Ks, 12 sub-machine guns and four I. MGs (light machine guns). A section comprised an officer, six NCOs and 42 soldiers. (BA 101 I 198/1384/11)

Landsers walking in a file. Three 8.1-cm mortar bases can be made out, carried on the men's backs. The tactical sign of a company can also be distinguished, painted on the rear of the cart. There was only one cart like this in each infantry section.
(BA 101 I 198/1384/14)

Generalleutnant Hans Frhr. Von Funck was born on 23 December 1891 at Aachen. At 24 he took part in WWI as an artilleryman and officer cadet. After the conflict, he was one of the 100 000 soldiers of the Reichswehr and was recruited again in April 1939 with the rank of Oberst. He commanded an armoured regiment in 5. Pz.Div. At the beginning of 1941 he was promoted to Generalmajor and Kdr. of 7. Pz.Div. which he only left in December 1943 with the rank of Generalleutnant. Appointed General der Panzertruppe, he next commanded an infantry corps, the XXIII. A.K. then again Panzers when he took command of the famous XXXXVII Pz. Korps in March 1944. His principal awards were the Knight's Cross on 15 July 1941, the German Gold Cross on 14 March 1943 and the Oak Leaves after the Battle of Kursk. He died on 14 February 1979.
(Photo J. Charita. Coll. D.L.)

to advance. At the end of the afternoon, a Russian battalion emerged from a balka (valley). It headed straight for Hill 614 held by 3./Gren. Rgt. 326. Fortunately, the German guards gave the alert. In less than a minute, the Landsers were ready to welcome the enemy who, when they attacked the Germans, were surprised to have to attack under heavy fire. They had thought that the Grenadiere were entrenched further up, on the heights. The attack very quickly broke up in disorder with the officers desperately trying to reorganise their soldiers. Runaways were gunned down without compunction until order was restored and the human waves finally resumed the attack under fire from the Landsers' machine guns; the latter were soon ordered to fix bayonets. The Russians fought like devils to conquer the 3.Kp. positions, but after an hour of the bloodiest fighting, they were forced to give up and fall back whence they came. Bodies were littered all over the flat, dull countryside swept by the Grenadiere's fire.

The Russian attack which was carried out at 21.30 against 5. and 7./Gren. Rgt. 326 failed in exactly the same way. All the messages sent by Generalmajor von Horn who was formerly on the staff of 7. Pz.Div. finished with: *"We're holding!"*

Old Generalmajor von Funck gave out orders to his unit commanders then wished them SoldatenGlück (soldier's luck). Their mission was to go to the rescue of the Panzergrenadiere still fighting in the forest situated to the north of Miassoyedovo. The ebullient Oberstleutnant Schülz was chosen to lead this attack. This time the Werfers, together with the divisional artillery pieces, fired salvo after salvo in order to start a rolling barrage out in front of the Panzers.

When the German tanks got near the forest, a tornado of fire and steel fell upon them. Explosions echoed around the Panzergruppe's tanks. A Pz. III was hit, then a second…

The CO of II./Pz.Rgt. 25 spotted tank turret outlines just sticking up above ground level. *"Sakrament! They've buried their tanks!"* he yelled over the radio to Oberstleutnant Schülz who was coming up to identify the anti-tank guns which were targeting them from Hill 213.7.

Oberst Wirkler of the artillery regiment had a deeply-lined face and a sparkling look. He was struggling against fatigue. *"Save your ammunition, we'll soon run out if we carry on at this rate. We're going have to limit ourselves to artillery barrages coordinated with the Panzergruppe's advance."* he thundered to his group commanders who were disfigured from lack of sleep.

Unlike most of the other tanks of this type, this one has no Schürzen (skirt) protecting the running gear or the turret. At Kursk, the Panzer IV was the most powerful tank in service with the three Pz. Div. of III. A. K. The shells fired from the 75 Kwk L/48 canon could pierce all Soviet armour.

After a barrage which blasted even the Russian tanks which were dug in up to their turrets, those which survived moved to the rear.

Panzergruppe Schülz fought on till nightfall; so did the Panzergrenadiere from 7. Pz.Div., who only succeeded in investing half the forest.

THE 19. PZ.DIV. SECTOR

At 9.30, the remnants of 19. Pz.Div. left the Delnazhaya Yigumenka sector to head northwest. Objective: Kissolovo.

In early afternoon, the roads along which 19. Pz.Div. was progressing were covered in a thick layer of dust. The combatants needed a rest.

"*We are going to start attacking again,*" announced Generalleutnant Schmidt to his unit commanders. "*We're going to take Kisselovo after a heavy preparatory barrage from the artillery*"

The plan was the following: Oberstleutnant Richter's Pz.Gren.Rgt.74 and Gren. Rgt. 442 were to attack from the east along a crest; Pz.AA 19 under Major Wilmsen would go round the town and attack from the west. Then Pz.Gren.Rgt.73 would attack the northern part of the town.

These shock troops got going without encountering any opposition but then after an hour, the Russian artillery opened fire for all it was worth.

The tanks from Panzergruppe Westoven supporting the Panzergrenadiere under Major Horst arrived within sight of the first houses of Kisselovo. They were

Leutnant Walter Riedel commanded 3./Pz.Gren.Rgt. 73 during the Battle of Kursk. He was awarded the Knight's Cross on 14 April 1943.
(Photo J. Charita. Coll. D.L.)

about to be hugely disappointed. Oberstleutnant Richter's Panzergrenadiere who ought to have taken part in the attack were not present. They were stopped by a minefield. More than 800 mines had to be removed in their sector before they could join up with Westoven's forces.

"*We don't have time to wait for the 74th. We'll attack now.*" Major Horst made his decision. A short while afterwards, the first explosions of the Panzers' 75-mms,

relayed by the sharp bursts from the MG 34s were to be heard. The heavy mortar shells also fell on Melikhovo. The Russian artillery replied instantly. Its guns, placed on the heights, fired at the attackers' flanks. The Stukas from VIII. FliergerKorps appeared very rapidly to take out the Russian gunners who, caught between the bombing and firing from the planes and from 19. Pz.Div.'s artillery were forced to abandon their guns and get under cover.

The Panzers and their accompanying infantry under Major Horst took advantage of all this to go past the enemy artillery positions and get as close to the town as possible.

Major Wilsem's Scouts had already run into the Russian infantry which had set themselves up behind barricades. Anti-tank guns had been positioned at the entrances and exits to the town which were soon crushed beneath 10.5-cm and 15-cm shells. Among all the ruins, any sector still resisting was surrounded and put out of action one after the other.

When Oberstleutnant Richter reached his soldiers, he encouraged them to finish off the last points where there was still any resistance.

After being re-supplied with ammunition and fuel, Westhoven's Panzers were ordered to hold themselves ready to advance with the support of Kampfgruppe 73 and Pz. AA 19. These units made up a bridgehead which was then to be used as the departure point for an attack northwards. Pz.Gren.Rgt.73 set off first.

While II./Pz.Gren.Rgt. 73's forces were fighting to capture Kissolovo, the Landsers in Gren. Rgt. 429 had taken the pressure off their rear by attacking the Russian 89th Guards Infantry Division. They succeeded in breaking through the Russian defences and then in investing the town of Petropavlovka after destroying a T-34. To the west of the river, Gren. Rgt. 417, having breached the 89th Guards Infantry Division's lines, took Belomestnazha and Hills 190.5 and 211.6. After all these achievements, Major Barkmann was ordered to clear

Left:
This volunteer from the East, originally from Kuban as shown by the insignia sewn carelessly onto his right sleeve is heating his mess tin. In a short time, he is going to help evacuate the wounded from this wood. His head and neck are covered by a mosquito net. 1943 was a turning point for these Russians who had come out of the prisoner of war camps so that they could fight communism. There were 800 000 of them, but some of their battalions turned out not to be very reliable and Hitler disbanded several of them, sending 80 000 of these volunteers to France.
(BA 198/1394/20)

out the woods to the north of the town. There his men encountered resistance of a completely different mettle. When he gave the signal for the last assault, the Grenadiere came under fire from the undergrowth. They responded, still advancing into this wood which seemed to be teeming with soldiers. After an engagement lasting 15 minutes, they discovered that the Russians were trying to take them in a pincer movement.

Major Barkmann gathered together his company commanders and ordered them to destroy this network of fortifications by launching three attacks at the same time. The heavy companies already in position would support them. He added one final recommendation. *"Coordination among our units is of paramount importance. We cannot allow ourselves to let a company get itself isolated."*

At the signal, the Landsers went into action. One of their groups managed to surprise the enemy on his right flank and succeeded in eliminating the first strong points. A second slipped through the trees like shadows and attacked the enemy with bayonets, grenades and MP40s. After about ten minutes of hand to hand fighting, the Landsers had to get out in a hurry because the Russians were continually bringing in reinforcements which they had been holding in reserve. These reinforcements soon charged the Germans who fell back leaving a protective screen behind them. This was a sacrificial mission which enabled the assault groups to regain their starting points.

Major Barkmann ordered his officers to get their men to dig individual foxholes as there was no question of starting another attack for the time being. In the end his regiment got the better of the Russian resistance by skirting round his defensive networks and fighting hand to hand in the first light of dawn.

CONCLUSION CONCERNING THE DAY OF 11 JULY 1943 IN THE III. PZ.KORPS SECTOR

Generalfeldmarschall von Manstein's excellent strategy together with

Gen. d. Pz. Tr. Breith's skills, and the initiative and the courage of his troops resulted in OKW's attention being riveted on III. Pz.Korps' advance.

When Stalin learnt of the not very enviable situation in which his 69th Russian Army found itself, he understood that it had to react immediately.

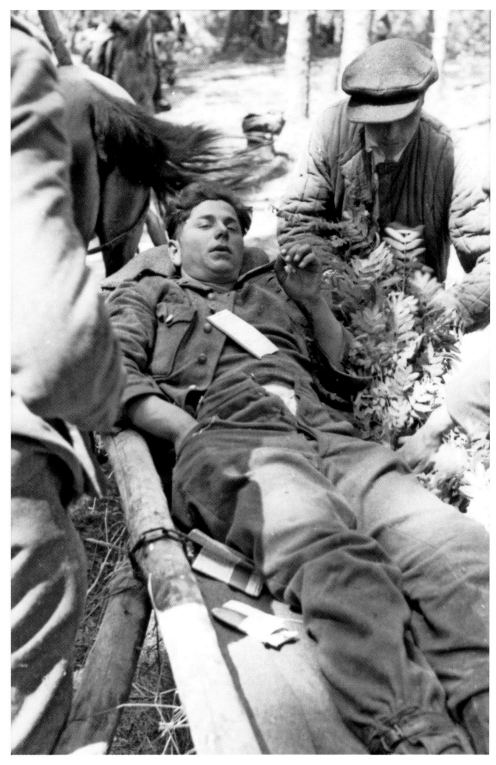

Above:
The wounded found themselves often in very difficult circumstances before being evacuated by the personnel from the medical companies. Sometimes they had to wait for hours on the battlefield or in the woods as was the case here. Many died before being looked after. On the first day of the offensive, one medical company section from of 19. Pz.Div. alone cared for 413 wounded. Among the divisions engaged in Operation Citadel, the infantry suffered the most casualties. For only 11 July 1943, 198.I.D. lost 111 soldiers and for the period 11 to 17 July, it lost 474 men. These heavy losses are not only to be accounted for by the bitterness of the fighting but also by the absence of field hospitals behind this division's front. The wounded were only evacuated on 13 July by medical teams directly from III. Pz.Korps.
(BA 101 I/198/1394/21a)

Indeed, Breith's armoured group could at any moment appear suddenly to the rear of the 5th Army (850 tanks) which was facing II.SS-Pz.Korps in front of Proshorovka…

In order to preserve the 69th Army which was staggering under the blows from the III. Pz.Korps battering ram,

General Watutin sent the 375th division to the Rindinka-Shipi sector where Pz.Rgt. 27 of 19. Pz.Div. was operating.

Conscious that the enemy must not have a moment's respite in which to regroup, Gen. d. Pz. Tr. Breith ordered his 6. Pz.Div. to get hold of Rshavezhh and to set up a bridgehead there.

Hauptmann Gustav Reimarr who led 6./Pz.Gren.Rgt. 4 during Operation Citadel fought in the ranks of the unquestioned master in matters of tactics, Oberst Unrein. Reimarr was awarded the Knight's Cross on 28 July 1943. He fell in battle on 23 March 1945 in Hungary.
(Photo J. Charita. Coll. D.L.)

ering role towards the east, in the region of Kasatzh.

The Trufanov group, comprising the 26th Armoured Guards Brigade and the 11th and 12th Motorised Guards Brigade, appeared to the north of Armee-Abteilung Kempf. It then went off in the direction of the Donets, threatening Gen. d. Pz. Tr. Breith's plan. He contacted VIII. FliegerKorps for it to intervene and halt the Russian advance, and also give air cover to the troops who had to take Rshavezh. In order to get hold of this town, the Kdr. of Pz.Rgt. 11 got together his last two companies and Hauptmann Graf von Kageneck's last Tigers which were stationed at Kasatzh together with a battalion from Pz.Gren.Rgt.4.

It was midnight when the Panzerkampfgruppe set off for Rshavezh. The crews were having a lot of trouble staying awake.

Craftily, Oberst von Oppeln Bronikowski placed two *"borrowed"* T-34s at the head of his column so that they could get through the defences unheeded. Any confrontation before getting to the objective was of no use.

The column seems to have been made up in the following way. 7./Pz.Rgt. 11 opened the way, followed by 7./Pz.Gren.Rgt. 114, then by

8./Pz.Rgt. 11, then by the rest of II./Pz.Gren.Rgt. 114 (Hauptmann Necknauer's SPW battalion.) Finally the Tigers brought up the rear.

The moonless night considerably helped this "armoured commando" which

Hauptmann Erich Oeckel, Kdr. of I./Pz.Gren.Rgt. 114 (6. Pz.Div.) was killed on 13 July 1943 near Rshavezh; he was awarded the Knight's Cross on 24 June 1940 when he was commanding officer of 5./Schtz.Rgt.4.
(Photo J. Charita.)

advanced without any hindrance. After moving for three hours, von Oppeln Bronikowski's column crossed Kurakovka without opposition then ran into a convoy of Russian trucks which it patiently allowed to pass on its way.

A four o'clock, Leutnant Huchtmann sallied out on reconnaissance in the

Occupying this terrain would give III. Pz.Korps a springboard from which it would be able to launch itself westwards in the direction of Lvov. On the other hand, 7. Pz.Div. would continue its cov-

This Marder III, with its Pak 40 mounted in the centre of the vehicle is from the middle of the series. Later the combat compartment was placed further back on the hull in order to balance out the tank better. Mounted on a Panzer 38(t) chassis, this formidable tank buster had inadequate armour on its superstructure: 8 to 10 mm.

eastern sector of Rshavezh with the remnants of 5./Pz.Rgt. 11, roughly the equivalent of a section. He followed Unteroffizier Franz Frank's tank, a T-34 painted with a Balkenkreuz. In spite of the large number of guards, convoys and horse-drawn carts, his armoured group managed to pass through unhindered. Then they arrived in sight of a bridge which was being crossed by Russian tanks overloaded with infantrymen. Keeping his head, Leutnant Huchtmann waited patiently for them to pass him. The Russians did not pay any attention to him. Meanwhile, Major Bäke had got down from his tank to listen to the report from *"Texas Franz"*. Ex-Obergefreiter Kordt takes up the tale.

"He suggested that we didn't speak"

The tension reached its climax when Leutnant Huchtmann's T-34 broke down right in the middle of the road, right in front of the well-entrenched Russian positions. For the time being the enemy had not noticed anything.

Ex-Obergefreiter Kordt who was next to Major Bäke at that moment still remembers him speaking to Leutnant Huchtmann on the radio: *"Breathe deeply and count the tanks!"* The Major turned to us informing us that there were 22 T-34s near the Leutnant, then he ordered us to wait for a while! A short time after this forced break, Bäke's tanks headed for the river. The Germans took advantage of the effect of surprise when they opened fire on the Russian tanks.

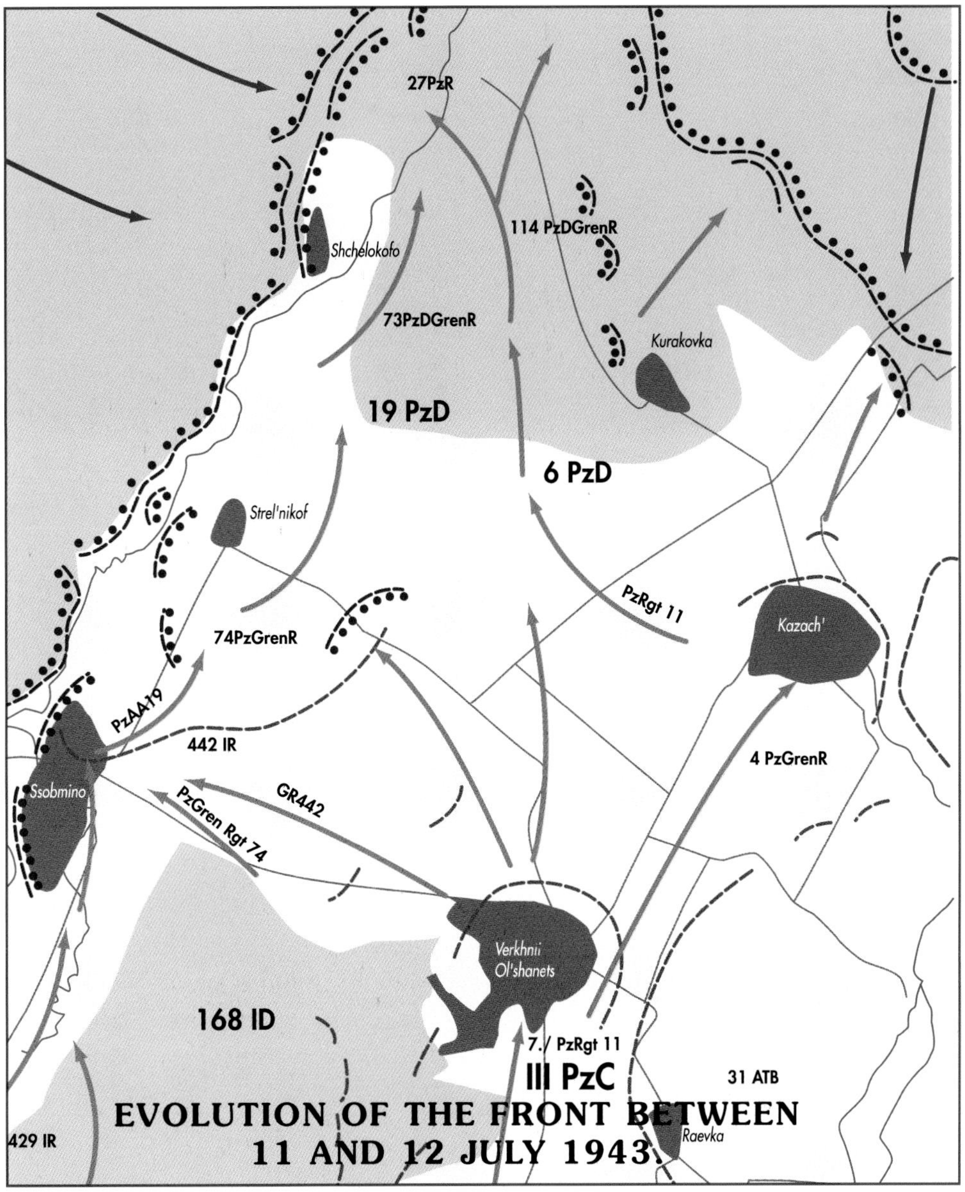

Major Bäke and his adjutant Leutnant Zobel destroyed ten T-34s and one T70 just between the two of them! The Panzerschützen rushed in to the fray and on the way captured four anti-tank positions which did not have time to fire a single shot. Two Stalin's organs and other vehicles were also destroyed. Their tanks got to less than three hundred yards from the bridge when it went up in a huge explosion. Gradually the cloud of smoke disappeared revealing the remains of the bridge. By some miracle the Sappers were able to get it operational again.

This operation has been reconstructed using the KTB, the divisional history of 6. Pz.Div., the personal memoirs of Oberst von Oppeln Bronikowski and titbits of information from different archives. On the whole there is agreement about the way things went, but there are discrepancies with some of the details, in particular with Major Dr Bäke's narrative which comes from his diary (published by the Historian Franz Kurowski). It is left up to the rea-

EVOLUTION OF THE FRONT BETWEEN 11 AND 12 JULY 1943

Map labels: 27PzR, 114 PzDGrenR, Shchelokofo, 73PzDGrenR, Kurakovka, 19 PzD, 6 PzD, Strel'nikof, PzRgt 11, Kazach', 74PzGrenR, PzAA19, 442 IR, 4 PzGrenR, Ssobmino, GR442, PzGren Rgt 74, Verkhnii Ol'shanets, 168 ID, 7./ PzRgt 11, III PzC, 31 ATB, 429 IR, Raevka

der to appreciate and decide. *"A T-34 led the way. I ordered radio silence and especially no shooting. We crossed the lines silently, then the first anti-tank defences which remained calm because the Red Army soldiers thought we were friendly.*

"When our T-34 broke down because of engine trouble, a Panzer IV replaced it at the head of the column. Rshavezh appeared in front of us. Near the town there were some T-34 crews who thought we belonged to the same unit as them and that we were returning from the front. Suddenly a column of enemy tanks turned up going in the opposite direction. Leutnant Huchtmann who was in the leading tank counted 22 T-34s, practically one behind the other. Suddenly six or seven of them left the column and going back where they had come from, got into line behind us. I ordered the column to keep going then I placed my own command tank which was only armed with a false canon across the road, forcing the seven enemy tanks to stop in front of me almost in a semi-circle.

"I called my operations officer and asked him to bring me some hollow explosive charges. We discreetly left my tank then reaching the group of tanks we placed a charge on two of the machines and ran for cover. The explosions tore through the night. Two T-34s had just been destroyed. We took another two charges and repeated the operation, so that a short while later two more T-34s were put out of action and then a fifth one by one of our Panzers."

Oberst von Oppeln Bronowski confirms that he launched himself with his group of Panzers at the rest of the Russian column and that the last Russian tanks blew up the bridge before pulling back.

Without waiting for their comrades from the SPW battalion who only arrived at 5 o'clock, the men from I./Pz.Gren.Rgt. 114 set up a bridgehead on the other side of the Donets. The capture of Rshavezh enabled III. Pz.Korps to launch its attack towards the west, according to the plan and to take the Russians from the rear.

THE EIGHTH AND LAST DAY OF OPERATION CITADEL: 12 JULY 1943

If III. Pz.Korps managed to join up with II.SS-Pz.Korps on its eastern flank, Generaloberst Hoth's 4. Pz. Armee would be able to break the Russian 6th Army with its XXXXVIII Pz. Korps; this Korps would then reach Obozhan, with the Russian 5th Army caught in a noose between III. Pz.Korps and II.SS-Pz.Korps.

With that in mind, 7. Pz.Div. was the division designated to make contact with II.SS-Pz.Korps. In order to give it more freedom of movement, General-major von Horn's 198.I.D. relieved it at the end of the afternoon where it was positioned in the Razumnoe Valley, between Miassoyedovo and Kalinina. Generalmajor von Funck therefore had his units go through Melikhovo to reach Kasatzh which had been chosen as the departure point for the following attack. He had however to leave an armoured company and an artillery group from his division at Jastrebovo.

The plan seemed to be feasible but Trufanov's group, which was heading towards the bridgehead set up by

6. Pz.Div., was posing a serious threat to the plan…

To begin with, the remainder of 7. Pz.Div. had to meet up with 6. Pz.Div. before launching the attack. Large Russian reinforcements coming from the north had arrived during the morning. 25 tanks had been spotted. The towns of Novo Alexezhevki, Visselok and Alexandrovka were transformed into strongholds by the Russians.

Alarming news was transmitted to Gen. d. Pz. Tr. Breith's HQ: the Russians had launched an offensive against XI.A.K. which up until now had been covering the rear of III. Pz.Korps.

Major Quentin of Pz. AA. 6 – who was responsible for protecting 6. Pz.Div.'s flank in the Schlachovozhe sector –

waited in vain for the elements from 7. Pz.Div. to arrive; they were due to relieve his battalion. As a safety precaution, he ordered his Scouts to return towards Kalinina.

Ordered to repel the Russian 96th Tank Battalion which was approaching Alexandrovka, Pz.Rgt. 25 left Kasatzh immediately. As a result, 7. Pz.Div. was left all by itself to face any Russian attacks and under constant threat of attack on its totally exposed flanks. II./ Werfer Regiment 52, Flak Abt.91 and II./Art. Rgt. 62 were attached to it to give

Above:
Model 43 T-34/76s. Note the tree trunk on the side mudguard which was regularly used to get the tank out of the mud on Russian roads.
(DR Caption by M. Chaubiron)

by Bild-Berichter Wolf-Allvater from P.K.637 (ECPAD DAT 3012)

Left: Three personalities from 3./s. Pz.Abt. 503 in full discussion: from left to right: Leutnant Weinert, commanding the third section; Oberfeldwebel Burgis and Oberfähnrich Rondorf. Although all three of them belonged to the armoured arm and even to the same unit, they are all wearing different jackets. Weinert has retained the double-breasted black tunic o the Panzerwaffen. Burgis is wearing the rush green combat jacket and Rondorf, the camouflage jacket on which he has pinned his Iron Cross, First Class. The metal insignia of the outline of a Tiger can be seen on his Model 1943 cap. This was s. Pz.Abt. 503's insignia. (© ECPAD DAT 3012 - L04)

Left: Tiger 323 belonging to Oberfeldwebel Burgis going along the muddy track of a village. The situation is relaxed. All the crew members, except for the driver, are outside riding on the tank. The state of the track would seem to indicate that this scene took place in autumn or winter, when it was in fact in August 1943. On the ground, Oberleutnant Scherf watches his Tigers filing past him. (© ECPAD DAT 3012 - L 10)

Bottom left: Hauptmann Scherf congratulating Oberfähnrich Rondorff who had been awarded the Deutsch Kreuz in Gold. S. Pz.Abt. 503's metal insignia can be seen on Scherf's forage cap. (Photo: von Rosen. Coll. D.L.)

Below: The crew of Tiger 331 commanded by Oberfähnric Rondorf. He was one of the 3./s. Pz.Abt. 503 aces with 10(confirmed kills. (© ECPAD DAT 3012- L23

Above: *Feldwebel Gärtner on leave in 1944. It was the last time Gärtner would see his little son. He was killed in combat on 5 January 1945.* (Photo: von Rosen. Coll. D.L.)

Top left: *S. Pz.Abt. 503's second ace was Feldwebel Heinz Gärtner who scored 103 kills. On his left Gefreiter Klein.* (Photo: von Rosen. Coll. D.L.)

Left:ontre
Oberfeldwebel Sachs, an experienced Panzerkommandant, much appreciated by 3./s. Pz.Abt. 503's Panzerschützen. Here he is in the company of Feldwebel Weigl from Tiger 334. (Photo: von Rosen. Coll. D.L.)

These three Tigers from Leutnant von Rosen's section going down a tree-lined lane to fill up with petrol in a calmer setting. (© ECPAD DAT 3012- L24)

Above: *Grefreiter and machine gunner Klein was one of Feldwebel Gärtner's crew – Tiger 334 – from the unit's creation until the end of the war. Klein scuttled his Tiger II while they were moving up to the front and the bridgehead at Mantes in August 1944. Willi Klein died in 2004.* (Photo: von Rosen. Coll. D.L.)

Right: *A bit of a rest for Oberleutnant Scherf and his men. Although in shirt sleeves, the Kdr. of the 3.Kp. is nevertheless wearing the regulation tie. Leutnant Weinert, recognisable by his white scarf, has his back to the photographer. The Panzerschütze (awarded the Iron Cross, Second Class) who is holding his belt with his left hand is listening his superiors. As for the Oberfeldwebel in a smock with four pockets, he is wearing the Panzerkampfzeichen (tank engagement insignia) and a campaign ribbon. The officer wearing a trench-coat who is lying down does not belong to s. Pz.Abt. 503.*
(© ECPAD DAT 3012- L27)

Note 3./s. Pz.Abt. 503's tactical insignia painted on the rear left of the vehicle; note also the tactical insignia of III. Zug from 3./s. Pz.Abt. 503, a triangle/rectangle painted on the rear left of the same vehicle.
(© ECPAD DAT 3012- L25)

it the cover it need. The AA was to play a vital role against the numerous Russian air attacks.

Rshavezh was attacked in order several times by the Trufanov group. Each time the attacks were driven off by 7. and 8./Pz.Rgt. 11 who had been ordered to defend the town. At 18.00 fighting stopped. Three T-34s remained on the battlefield.

Oberst Unrein thought that the outer defences of Rshavezh were too weak and asked Hauptmann Malchowski to reinforce Pz. AA. 6 with his Sturmgeschütze.

The III. Pz.Korps units fought all day to keep the terrain which had been won the previous day. But a very big threat was looming in the Kurakovka-Alexandrovka sector, held by Kampfgruppe Unrein. The 92nd Guards Division drove in his line of defence in the hope of joining up with the 81st Guards Division situated to the north of the Donets. This manoeuvre would enable the Russians to encircle the 6. Pz.Div. and take back Rshavezh. The Russians' intention was confirmed when an armoured section under Oberfeldwebel Parhofer from 6. Pz.Div. reported powerful armoured forces at Alexandrovka.

Since 7.45, the Panzers from Pz.Rgt. 27 from 19. Pz.Div., the Kampfgruppen from 73rd and 74th Panzergrenadiere Regiments, and Pz. AA.19 had been trying to take Sabinino. An artilleryman from Pz.Art.Rgt. 19 tells the story. "The Panzers entered a field which went as far as Sabinino. Suddenly Russian tanks

Avec les éclaireurs de sa 3./Pz.AA. 6, l'Oberleutnant Fritz Biermann est rentré au cœur des lignes adverses et, à plusieurs reprises a ramené, des renseignements qui ont été décisifs pour la conduite des opérations de la 6. Pz.Div. Il est décoré de la Croix de chevalier après la bataille de Koursk. Il est tué le 30 mars 1945 en Hongrie. Il était alors Oberleutnant au Kradschützen-Btl. 6. Il avait obtenu la Croix allemande en or le 17 avril 1943. (Coll.: Josef Charita. Coll.: D.L.)

appeared. One of our tanks was hit and evacuated by its crew. The Grenadiere who had been riding on our tanks, rushed off towards the gardens in the village. When they reached the first houses, groups of Russians appeared and our men had to withdraw. We could

not support them with our guns as we were hindered by poor visibility."

Major Horst's Kampfgruppe succeeded in advancing because the resistance it came up against was not as determined as it was against the other 19. Pz.Div. units. This advance was made easier by the excellent cover to his right flank provided by Major Wilsem's Scouts.

On the other hand, Oberleutnant Richter's Panzergrenadiere were slowed down from the outset because they immediately came under fire from a heavy concentration of Russian artillery and anti-tank guns.

For one interminable hour, the artillery batteries from II. and III./Pz.Art.Rgt. 19 which had moved up the previous night, tried to outgun the Russian artillery which, under the constant fire from the 15-cms, was gradually silenced.

With very good support, Oberstleutnant Richter was able to reorganise his Kampfgruppe and then launch it back into the attack. Suddenly the thunder let loose. Opposite them, hidden in the forest and at just the right range for their weapons, the Russian infantry started shooting at them. But instead of throwing himself to the ground, Oberstleutnant Richter climbed on top of a mound so that his soldiers could see him easily and then urged them to attack the Russian positions He was convinced they would succeed.

When the Russians saw the highly enthusiastic and motivated Panzergrenadiere rushing towards them, they

Oberfelfwebel Burgis' Tiger 323.

could not believe their eyes. The Germans fought even more ferociously than before. Mad with boldness, they reached the Russian positions in groups and in less than ten minutes it was all over: the Germans had taken the positions.

Shortly afterwards, Oberstleutnant Richter was ordered to set up positions on the terrain captured by Pz. Gren.Rgt.73 which, after taking Sabini-no, had also captured Krivzovo and Strelnikoff; then at 14.15, he made contact with units of 6. Pz.Div. at Rshavezh.

At the end of the day, elements from 19. Pz.Div. relieved the 6. Pz.Div. units which had managed to set up a bridgehead at Rindinka. They now had to set up another bridgehead to the northwest of Visselok.

To Generalleutnant Schmidt's utter amazement a new, fresh unit reached the front. This was Marsch-Btl. z.b.v. Tr.

Above: *Followed by infantry, these T-34s rush the enemy. In 1943, this tank was more mobile than any other medium tank, and even more mobile than light tanks. Its frontal armour was almost as thick as that on the Tiger. Its rate of fire however was mediocre and its penetration capability did not enable it to destroy a Tiger front on, even at short range.*
(DR Caption by M. Chaubiron)

T-34/76 Model 43. Not shown on this profile are the tree trunks which were often carried on the mudguards. They were used to get the tank out of the mud.

Left: *Lying in ambush in a field situated near a house, the gun commander is scrutinising the land through his binoculars. Near him, in fatigue dress, the driver seems relaxed. The third server cannot be seen. This Marder II, armed with a Pak 40 75-mm gun, was a formidable tank buster. It equipped only the Panzerjäger-Abteilungen of the armoured divisions. 2./Pz.Jg.Abt. 41 only was equipped with Marder IIs. It had nine of them. 1. Kp. had nine Marder IIIs and the 3. Kp. had two sections of Flak 2-cms and a section of Flak-Vierling. Pz.Jg.Abt. 19 which was equipped with 12 Marders on 4 July 1943 lost three of them during the first three days it was engaged. 7. Pz.Div. lost only one.* (© ECPAD DAT 3017 - L2)

Bottom left:
Judging by the state of his rush green combat dress and the state of the Marder, these men have most certainly been fighting for several days now. The Unteroffizier and tank commander is handing a document to the driver. The rear view of the tank shows that the crew has completely covered the rear with tent canvas. Maize stalks have been stuck onto the Marder's flanks on which a helmet with its camouflaged protective covering has been hung.
(© ECPAD DAT 3017 - L3)

Below:
Struggling under the weight, this Grenadier is bringing back five water containers for his comrades. This group of soldiers is probably threatened with encirclement. For information, 168.I.D. lost 2 623 men (of which 420 killed) between 4 and 20 July 1943, a total of 30% of the overall losses for III. Pz.Korps.
(© ECPAD DAT 3017- L9)

DOCUMENTARY REPORT WITH III. PZ.KORPS
by bild berichter Vorpahl from P.K. 637
(637th Propaganda Compagny) *(© ECPAD)*

Sheltering in a multi-storeyed building, these Grenadiers are recovering for few hours which they spend cleaning their weapons. They have placed Kanisters full of water near the right hand wall. Note also the field telephone wire running along the wall of the room. The weapon belts have been put here and there, but the water flasks and quarts are near the men.

(© ECPAD DAT 3017- L5)

This Funker has prudently set up his radio transmitter in a ditch for pipes or electric cables. In an emergency, he can cover his shelter with the thick plank next to him. He has put his notepad on his camouflage tent canvas so that he can take notes during a call. The section commander is lying down near him so that he can be on hand to receive any radio messages or to answer questions from his superiors. He is wearing a camouflaged cotton tunic with chevrons.

(© ECPAD DAT 3017- L7)

Previous page top left: *This infantryman is looking round the premises holding his Mauser ready in his hand. The building has suffered from the fighting, witness the impacts along the walls.* (© ECPAD DAT 3017 - L 10)

Previous page top Right: *The NCO seen above talking to his superior. The particular cut of the camouflaged jacket suggests that he is most certainly wearing the Heer's rare Tarnjacke, issued mainly to the Gross Deutschland Division. The officer on the right, an Oberleutnant, is wearing the combat dress for ordinary soldiers on which he has sewn his attributes. The dark edges on his early head dress, an Alter Art, could be red, the colour of the artillery.* (© ECPAD DAT 3017- L13)

Previous page bottom: *Aboard an Sd Kfz.251/11 mittlere Fernsprechpanzerwagen, the Regimental Kdr., an Oberst, has just visited the company which has set up its defences around the building. He has been awarded the Deutsch Kreuz, the Iron Cross, First Class and probably the general assault insignia and the medal for the wounded. In this case it means that he was awarded a number of decorations over a period of time and during the course of several campaigns as confirmed by the width of the bar pinned above his left pocket flap. The other two people in the half-track at the rear are both wearing headphones. The fox-terrier following the colonel on his rounds could be the regimental mascot.* (© ECPAD DAT 3017- L14)

Top right : *Monocle screwed into his right eye, the Oberst poses proudly for the camera in a posture which could be only be described as aristocratic. His driver, a simple Obergefreiter at the wheel of the Mercedes-Benz L 1500A, seems less at ease.* (© ECPAD DAT 3017- L15)

Right: *The company commander (2nd from right) appreciating this moment of relaxation with the regimental commander and the three section commanders. None of the latter has been awarded any decorations. This is clearly a recently formed unit.* (© ECPAD DAT 3017- L17)

Below: *A young Grenadier wearing a forage cap in a position defended by two machine guns, an MG 34 and an MG 42. The sheath for the spare barrel of one of the machine guns has been placed near the MG 42. Further away, the ovoid offensive stick grenades are among the items of the Heer soldier's personal equipment: water flask, bread bag, mess tin and gas mask. On the left of the photograph the metal case holding the 7.92-mm machine gun cartridge belts.* (© ECPAD DAT 3017- L19)

Above:
These mortar servers have dug their positions near a maize field. The heat is unbearable and their position uncomfortable. The 8-cm Granatwerfer 34 had a maximum range of one and a half miles. With its firing rate of 15 to 25 rounds a minute, it was a very effective support weapon. This model, adopted by the Heer as early as 1934, was produced until the end of the war. During the summer of 1943, there were generally one, or even two mortars, per infantry company in 6. Pz.Div.
(© ECPAD DAT 3017- L21)

Left:
A quite comfortable headquarters site has been set up on the side of the hill. As it is fine, the officers have taken the table and chairs out of their bunker which is only a few yards away. Two observers are positioned halfway up the hill, at the entrance to their hideout. One of them seems to be asleep judging by the position of his feet... Two 98Ks and a helmet are lying on the ground, outside the post. Everything seems to be in order, but is this not the calm before the storm? If one looks carefully at these posts, it becomes clear that air attacks were greatly feared everywhere.
(© ECPAD DAT 3017- L24)

121. Up until now, the strength of 19. Pz.Div. had totalled 12 024 soldiers (not counting the March Battalion) against 13 780 on 1 July 1943.

To the west of the river, the Landsers from Gren. Rgt. 417 had spent part of the night in the forest fighting elements of the Russian 89th Guards Infantry Division. They attacked again at dawn of 12 July. From the unit's log book: *"At several points in the forest, the regiment encountered heavy resistance which it was only able to reduce after furious hand to hand fighting. When I./Gren. Rgt. 417 reached the northern edge, it rushed off in the direction of another wood situated a mile and a half away to the southeast of Gostishchevo. But the approaches to this wood were protected by a line of bunkers."*

Led by their company commanders, the Landsers took these positions after moving up through a barrage of fire where several of them fell.

The Russian battalion commander was killed. One of his subordinates tried to rally the infantry which was near to panicking. Some of them rushed towards the Gostishchevo forest dropping their weapons on the way. *"200 prisoners were taken and the dead were no longer counted,"* concluded this unit's report. Gostishchevo became the centre of a hurricane when the Landsers from Gren. Rgt. 417 attacked and silenced the weak Russian defence. The command of the 89th Guards Infantry Division did not think that the Germans had got so deep into its division's lines.

Above: *Generalleutnant von Horn (left) seems to be exposing the situation of his 198.I.D. to General Speidel (centre) and Gen. d. Pz. Tr. Kempf (right). Although his division was only horse-drawn, it conducted itself and fulfilled its tasks with brio.*
(BA 22/2923/01)

Hoping beyond reason, Major Barkmann and his soldiers appeared in the Russian rear situated to the west of the river and then succeeded in attacking by surprise, crushing their positions.

When Generalmajor Chales de Beaulieu learnt the news, he asked the Kdr. of Gren. Rgt. 417 to hold Gostishchevo with enough men and then cross the river with the bulk of his regiment. His objective was to wipe out the last Russian units facing Gren. Rgt. 429.

Caught in the pincer movement, the Russians had no choice but to retreat northwards. This was carried out in disorder, enabling Gren. Rgt. 417 to set up a defensive line between Sabinino and Kisselovo. This released Gren. Rgt. 429 which was ordered to join Panzergruppe Bäke which itself had been ordered to attack Alexandrovka.

In turn the infantrymen from the Russian 89th Guards Infantry Division attacked the elements defending Gostishchevo. The Gren. Rgt. 417 Landsers were cut off from Gren. Rgt. 429 which was now situated to the east of the Donets. They risked running out

JSU 152. This impressive assault gun, fitted with a 152-mm howitzer appeared in 1943. It turned out to be an excellent tank buster, capable of standing up to the Tiger. Its rate of fire was slow however and its range shorter than the German 88.

Generalleutnant von Horn was born in East Prussia in 1896 and took part in WWI as an officer cadet. At the end of that conflict he was an ordnance officer and managed to stay in the Reichswehr. When the next conflict broke out, he was military attaché at the embassy in Paris. He was very quickly appointed chief-of-staff of XII.A.K., on 8 September 1939; he then kept the same post in X.A.K. on 1 June 1940. From July 1943 to February 1943, he occupied various training posts and temporarily replaced several unit commanders, the most important of which was that of CO of the Army of the Don. From 7 February 1943 to 1 June 1944, Generalleutnant von Horn commanded 198.I.D. He was then military attaché again at the embassy in Bern. Captured by the British in May 1945, he was freed in September 1947. He joined the Bundeswehr and became the CO of the National Defence. He retired in 1961. He was awarded the German Gold Cross on 1 December 1943. (DR.)

of supplies and ammunition. However, while they were getting ready to face the Russian assault at the beginning of the evening, the Signals were trying to set up a link with the divisional headquarters post.

The Russian infantry was supported by tanks from the 148th Armoured Brigade when they went over to the attack. Driven off, they went back to their jump-off positions and started off again deploying over a front which got narrower as it approached Gostishchevo.

The Red Army lost a great number of infantry on the battlefield but the tanks got away unscathed. Soon the isolated Gren. Rgt. 417 was forced to withdraw

if it was to escape the noose which was tightening around it on all sides. The most seriously wounded could not be evacuated. All around the Landsers, the earth was blackened by the exploding shells. Greatly outnumbered and with the enemy hard on their heels, they managed to reach the forest they had cleared out at dawn. They set themselves up in the former Russian positions and got ready for combat. All around them, the countryside seemed hostile, teeming with combat groups from the 89th Guards Infantry Division which started to move up along the lanes under cover of the forest. But all the Russian attacks failed.

Crouching at the bottom of their positions, the Grenadiers were then bombarded by the enemy artillery, then by aircraft. The shells and bombs rained down on these soldiers who turned themselves into moles, trying to dig themselves into the ground. During the night the fighters came over strafing at low altitude.

Although the day had been very trying for all the III. Pz.Korps armoured divisions, it had also been gruelling for 198.I.D. Taking advantage of the darkness (11-12 July), Oberstleutnant Grassmann's Gren. Rgt. 305, preceded by an engineer company, set up a defensive line near a wood situated a mile and a half from Sevrzhukovo. Its III. Btl. remained at the rear, in reserve, near the Kdr.'s HQ.

The darkness was so complete that there were no Russian aircraft that night. At about 3 a.m., a section from

Below:

Major Grassmann was in command of II./Gren. Rgt. 326 before taking command of Gren. Rgt. 305 for the Battle of Kursk. These two battalions relieved 198.I.D. He was awarded the Knight's Cross on 9 November 1942. General Speidel came to congratulate him for his Grenadiers' bravery in combat. (BA 22/2923/11)

Right:
The Führer presenting the Knight's Cross to Oberleutnant Theodor Tolsdorff (shaking hands with Hitler) from 14./Inf.Rgt.22 on 19 September 1943. From left to right: Oberst Schülz, Oberleutnant Lange from Pz.Gren.Rgt.73, Major Günther Pape, Kdr. of Pz.Gren.Rgt. 394 and Major Bäke of II./Pz.Rgt. 11. (Photo: J. Charita. Coll. D.L.)

Below:
Oberst Schülz watching a sporting event. Paul Schülz was born on 30 October 1891 at Tübingen. He was already a Leutnant in the infantry when WWI broke out. Between the wars, he served in the police then in 1935 joined the Heer. He was given command of II./Inf.Rgt.25 with the rank of Major. He became an Oberstleunant in October 1937, Oberst in September 1940 and Generalmajor in March 1944. As of 10 October 1944 he was in command of the 8. Armee Waffenschule. (Photo J. Charita. Coll. D.L.)

Oberst Schulz, Kdr. of Gren. Rgt. 308 of 198.I.D. added the Oak Leaves to his Knight's Cross on 24 July 1944 in the following circumstances: the enemy was carrying on its attacks with tank support. Gren. Rgt. 308 and one company from Gren. Rgt. 305 were taking the brunt of the attack. At the beginning, the Grenadiere pushed the enemy infantry back but when the enemy tanks were brought in to support them they were overwhelmed, since by firing at the flanks the tanks were helping the infantry assault groups to pierce the lines, but only after heavy fighting though. On his own initiative, Oberst Schulz organised a counter-attack with Gren. Rgt. 308. Two Sturmgeschütze which just happened to be in the sector took part in the operation. The enemy quickly fell back losing several tanks. The positions had barely been reoccupied when another part of the front yielded under Russian pressure. Once again, Oberst Schülz led a counter-attack. The enemy maintained its pressure and got reinforcements to come up so as to overwhelm Gren. Rgt. 308's positions. The battlefield echoed with the sound of tanks firing. For the third time, the enemy broke through Oberst Schulz's lines and for the third time the regiment's Kdr. once again gathered together his last reserves and launched a counter-attack at the enemy, this time forcing them to withdraw. (Photo: J. Charita. Coll. D.L.)

2./Pz.Jg.Abt. 235 joined the regiment. Other Sappers from 1./Pi.Btl. 235 followed them. Everybody dreaded not being able to hold the front. The regiment found itself in the centre of 198.I.D.'s disposition between Gren. Rgt. 308 and 329. From 8.30 onwards the Russians tried to dislodge the Gren. Rgt. 308 Landsers from their positions set up the night before. The mortars, cannon and Stalin's organs were fired relentlessly at them.

The Russians had in no way decided to give up the terrain taken by 198.I.D. and at 11.30, they launched a terrible attack which caused Gren. Rgt.308 to suffer heavy losses. Its 1st and 5th companies were ready to defend the crossroads situated to the south of Batrazkazha Datscha, outnumbered two to one.

Under the deluge of shells, the Grenadiere nevertheless held fast but the bombardment was getting more and more accurate, lifting up huge mounds of earth which smothered the soldiers. Then it was the turn of 6./Gren. Rgt. 308 to fend off an assault by Russian infantry who hurled themselves at them screaming. It was by letting these attacking waves rush to within less than a hundred yards that the Landsers were able to cut swathes through their ranks, taking out entire sections.

Although Gren. Rgt. 308 had managed to hold its front line, the situation for Generalmajor von Horn's division was turning out to be more and more alarming. He knew that his men would not be able to hold out much longer if the Russians kept up their attacks.

The news coming in from the VIII. FliegerKorps was worrying too: reconnaissance planes had spotted enemy troop movements, crossing the river Koren. This meant that reinforcements were moving up to attack his infantry regiments in strength.

"We must do everything to stop them. If we look closely at the route they are taking, you can see that they are heading for a portion of our front line", Generalmajor von Horn announced to his chief-of-operations. "We must change the way our units have been spread out and reinforce those sectors most under threat."

Above:
A canon opens fire. 200 campaign artillery pieces equipped III. Pz.Korps (BA 198/1363/27a)

"Exactly. Let III./Gren. Rgt. 308 and 7./Gren. Rgt. 308 relieve II. and III./Gren. Rgt. 326 which are holding this road. Don't forget that the farming coopera- tive is the strongest point in our line of defence."

When the Landsers of the 308th took over their positions from the 326th, dozens of shells exploded in the centre of the front line. A short while afterwards, a terrible attack nearly crushed the whole disposition Gren. Rgt. 308 had just organised, exactly where II. Btl. joined III. Btl. Artillery

198.I.D.'s priority objective that day was to relieve 7. Pz.Div. in its positions. But its Gren. Rgt. 326 which was originally intended for this mission had to launch several attacks with its I.Btl. to recapture the Solovzhev Kolkhoz. It only managed to do this with the help of Pz.Art.Rgt. 25. This operation took all afternoon and used up a lot of ammunition.

Right:
With the help of his binoculars, an observer is reporting exactly where the enemy is to the radio operator next to him who transmits the information immediately to the battery personnel. The binocular tripod is resting on the parapet of the trench. (BA 198/1363/29a)

Right:
The operator and his comrade have just enough time to put their overcoats on before jumping to the campaign telephone. The information will be transcribed on the gridded map spread out in front of the soldier. He uses a compass to help him indicate the Russian positions. Once this task is carried out, he transmits the information about the new situation to headquarters in Morse. The regulation petrol lamp, also placed on the table gives a pale and unreal atmosphere to this shot. The advanced posts only rarely had electricity.
(BA 198/1363/33a)

With nightfall, the Grenadiers entrenched in the cooperative drove off attack after attack with the support of the tank busters from 14./ Gren. Rgt. 326.

The historian of 198.I.D. states that the losses of the 15th Guards Division were heavy and after two days of fighting for the Kolkhoz, its units stopped coming. *"A great number of prisoners had been taken and a 12.-cm battery had been annihilated. Our own losses were not so high, but among the comrades who had fallen, there were Oberleutnant Roth from 2.Kp., and Leutnant Held of 3.Kp."* As two of his three infantry regiments were in the line, Generalmajor von Horn could only send Gren. Rgt. 305 to relieve Kampfgruppe Glaesemer (at about 17.00) in the *"Forest of the woman with the shoe"* sector.

Below:
A T-34/76, probably a model 42 judging by the rounder shape of its turret. According to a report from Heersgruppe Sud, its army corps used 28 T-34s in the month of July 1943.
(DR Caption by M. Chaubiron)

HOW OPERATIONS DEVELOPED AFTER CITADEL

13 JULY 1943

Hope of victory for Gen. d. Pz. Tr. Breith seemed to be fading quickly. Nothing was going to plan. The day before, his divisions had marked time and today the situation was getting no better: his 7. Pz.Div. which had gathered together as ordered to reorganise and then to launch an attack westwards, had been engaged at the last minute and was now engaged in endless fighting, particularly at Ivanovka which was the hinge around which the Russian tanks could manoeuvre.

Generalmajor von Funck had to give up his idea of attacking with the remnants of 6. Pz.Div. The division was shrinking by the hour (four tanks were annihilated during the day at Rshavezh). Pz.Rgt. 11 had only 14 tanks left.

To relieve the pressure on 6. Pz.Div. and 7. Pz.Div., VIII FliegerKorps sent Heinkel IIIs to attack the Trufanov group.

It was now that the catastrophe occurred: the Luftwaffe pilots dropped part of their bomb load on the 6. Pz.Div. bridgehead, wounding 49 men and

killing 15, all of them senior officers and all of them vital for the command of this elite division. It was Hauptmann von Kageneck's HQ at Rshavezh which reported this tragic accident.

Among the various people killed or who were to die from their wounds, there were Generalmajor von Hünersdorf; Major von Bieberstein (R.K.), Kdr. of Pz.Gren.Rgt. 114; Hauptmann Oeckel (R.K.), Kdr. of I./Pz.Gren.Rgt. 114; and Oberleutnant Wagemann of StuG.Abt. 228.

Among the wounded were Oberst von Oppeln Bronikowski, Kdr. of Pz.Rgt. 11 (who was replaced by Major Dr Bäke, Kdr. of II./Pz.Rgt. 11 who himself handed over command of the rest of his Abteilung to Hauptmann Scheibert); Hauptmann Necknauer, Kdr. of II./Pz.Gren.Rgt. 114 and Hauptmann Jahn, Kdr. of I./Pz.Art.Rgt.

These officers' absence at the front at this crucial moment of the operation severely compromised the success of Operation Citadel for III. Pz.Korps. Generalfeldmarschall von Manstein opposed… Hitler who wanted to cancel the offensive because of problems

which had arisen in the Mediterranean sector. In order to solve them, the Führer wanted to withdraw some of the divisions that were engaged at Kursk. He had made his choice. He preferred to give up Kursk and save Sicily where the Allies had landed.

To the north, Generaloberst Model's 9. Armee had to forsake Kursk because it had to reorganise and protect its rear, particularly in the Orel sector where it was threatened by the Russian armies. From now on, he would be busy with what was happening in the north-east and no longer the south. Generalfeldmarschall von Manstein was furious. He was an ardent supporter of Operation Citadel and all he could see now was victory slipping through his fingers just at the moment when he was about to win… Even though his XXXXVIII. Pz. Korps was halted in the marshes situated to the south of Obojan and

Above:
The Red Army had a lot of armoured cars. This is a BA 20 judging by the commander's cupola-shaped hatch and the little turret fitted with a machine gun.
(DR Caption by M. Chaubiron)

although the breach between II.SS-Pz.Korps and III. Pz.Korps was getting bigger and bigger, he was still thinking of launching a simultaneous attack. He was sure he would win in the south.

With this in mind, Generalfeldmarschall von Manstein met with his Generals, Hoth and Kempf, to inform them of the orders he had received from Hitler and about the plan he wanted them to carry out. For him the Russians were beaten because their reserves were engaged. Now was the moment to move in for the kill, precisely the opposite of what Hitler thought. The Führer wanted Armee-Abteilung Kempf and the 4. Pz. Armee to remain where they were.

According to von Manstein, they had to be quicker off the mark than the Russian 1st and 6th Armoured Armies who risked launching a large attack on the east flank of Hoth's 4. Pz. Armee. He planned Operation "Roland" which consisted of annihilating the enemy to the south of Proshorovka with the remnants of the four armoured divisions together with a new one, recently arrived on the front, the Wiking Division.

While these preparations were under way, Hauptmann Scheibert, Kdr. of II./Pz.Rgt. 11, and Hauptmann Graf von Kageneck left Rshavezh to assemble near Kurakovka and attack Alexandrovka. It was agreed that the remnants of 7. Pz.Div. would protect their eastern flank.

Capturing this village had become of paramount importance. It would enable the armoured elements to head northeast and join up with 2.SS-Pz.Div. -Das Reich- in the Pravarot sector, to the south of Proshorovka.

If Operation Roland succeeded, all the Russian forces situated in the triangle formed by the two Donets rivers - the Lipowezh-Donets and the North Donets – would find themselves encircled. Thus the in-depth breach which had been made by the Russians at the beginning of Operation Citadel (between III. Pz.Korps and II.SS-Pz.Korps) would probably cost Watutin his 2nd Armoured Corps.

All now depended on what the Panzergruppe under Gen. d. Pz. Tr. Breith did. It was made up of 63 Panzers from the remnants of Pz.Rgt. 11, Pz.Rgt. 25 and Pz.Rgt. 27, the six remaining Tigers from s. Pz.Abt. 503

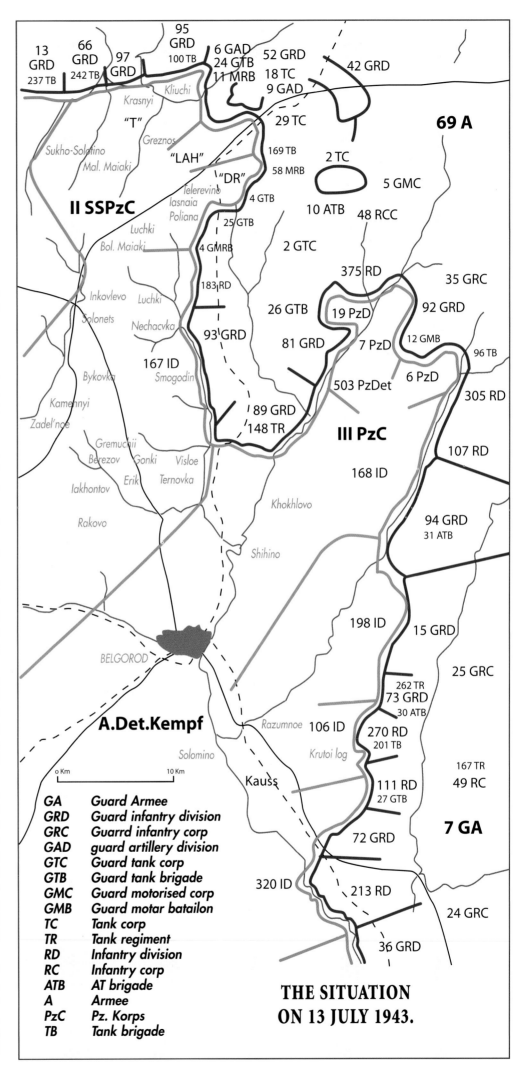

GA	Guard Armee
GRD	Guard infantry division
GRC	Guarrd infantry corp
GAD	guard artillery division
GTC	Guard tank corp
GTB	Guard tank brigade
GMC	Guard motorised corp
GMB	Guard motar batailon
TC	Tank corp
TR	Tank regiment
RD	Infantry division
RC	Infantry corp
ATB	AT brigade
A	Armee
PzC	Pz. Korps
TB	Tank brigade

THE SITUATION ON 13 JULY 1943.

DOCUMENTARY REPORT: NEBELWERFER IN ACTION

Above:

Nebelwerfer servers have just received orders to set up their piece as a battery. The gun is covered with a tarpaulin. The only Nebelwerfer unit attached to III. Pz.Korps was Werfer-Regiment 24 under Oberst Diedrich. Each of its three Abteilungen was equipped with eighteen 15-cm Nebelwerfers 41s. (BA 22/2943/11)

Above:

With rapid, accurate movements which reveal intensive training, these servers unhitch and then position their Nebelwerfer. This "cloud-maker" weighing 1 100 lb empty, was naturally moved around on its trailer by its servers. Once the six rockets were loaded, it weighed 1 694 lb. (BA 22/2943/13)

Right: *The tactical insignia of Werfer-Regiment 54 was two crossed swords, the emblem of the porcelain manufacturer, Meissemer. It was orchard green for the regiment but each of its three Abteilungen had a different colour: white for the first, red for the second and yellow for the third. The light columns had a vertical stripe under the tactical sign and the colour corresponded to that of the Abteilung to which it was attached.* (Source: Kameradchaft der ABC-Abwehr, Nebel und Nebel – und Werfertruppe)

Below:

The servers get the gun into position. The role of the Werfer was to bombard the enemy with its high-explosive shells or with special shells which prevented him from seeing anything by enveloping him in a dense cloud of artificial smoke. The first Werfers were issued at the end of 1940. (BA 22/2943/15)

Below:

The purveyors bring up the 15-cm Wurfgranate 41 Spreng HE heavy rockets, weighing 34.15 kg each (75.13 lb). The six rockets could be fired in ten seconds and three salvoes could be fired in three minutes. Their maximum range was just over four miles. They were fired electrically and the trigger was at the foot of the trail, on the right. (BA 22/2943/20)

Because there was no transport, like the Sd Kfz 251s or the half-tracks, in the Red Army the "motorised" infantry rode on the backs of tanks, as can be seen here.
(DR Caption by M. Chaubiron)

and the last 12 Strumgeschütze from StuG.Abt. 228.

But the offensive planned for taking Alexandrovka had to be delayed because of the numerous Russian attacks launched from the Rasumnaya valley. The enemy's objective was to break through the eastern flank of III. Pz.Korps in depth, i.e. in the 168.I.D. sector where two thirds of its forces, Gren. Rgt. 442 and Gren. Rgt. 229, were protecting the eastern flank of the armoured corps along the banks of the Rasumnaya between Scheino - Melikhovo (incl.) and Kasatzh.

Gren. Rgt. 442 defended the Komintern sector where there was an important bridge and Gren. Rgt. 429 occupied the ravine which went from Svischtev to the 442's bridge.

The Landsers' objective was to push the Russians back beyond the river if attacked, whilst at the same time maintaining contact with the east flank of 198.I.D. I./Flak Regiment 38 was the only back-up that Generalmajor Chales de Beaulieu could hope to get for his troops. As for Major Barkmann's Gren. Rgt. 417, it was exposed on the western flank of III. Pz.Korps in the Gostishchevoto - Strelnikov sector. Unlike what has been planned, 7. Pz.Div. limited itself to playing a defensive role facing the Russians which were advancing straight at the Sappers from Pz.Pi.Btl. 58 who were soon pinned down under a powerful

Oberst Wolgang Glaesemer, Kdr. of Pz.Gren.Rgt. 6. He was awarded the German Gold Cross on 21 February 1942 when he was in command of Inf. Rgt. 460, then the Knight's Cross on 12 February 1943. He took temporary command of 7. Pz.Div. between 17 and 20 August 1943.
(Photo J. Charita. Coll. D.L.)

artillery barrage.

II./Werfer Regiment 54's batteries

went into action two or three minutes later, thereby alerting the Grenadiere of II./Pz.Gren.Rgt. 74 attached to Oberst Glaesemer's Kgp. (Pz.Gren. Rgt.6). The exploding shells from the mittlerer Granatwerfer in this battalion merged with the sounds of the anti-tank rifles.

After a quarter of an hour, the Russian artillery lengthened its range. Oberst Glaesemer who only had his I. Btl. at his disposal, understood very quickly that his tactical group would be overwhelmed if it did not get back to the Werfer battery emplacements. He gave the order to fall back to his officers who got themselves organised immediately.

The Russians immediately rushed up and took over the positions abandoned by Glaesemer's Panzergrenadiere. They ran all over the place looking for resistance, but there was none to find. When Panzergrenadiere reached the heights where the Nebelwerfer emplacements were situated, they could make out the Russian infantry apparently reorganising for a resumption of their attack.

"What do we do now, Herr Oberst?" asked the adjutant. *"We're going to counter-attack, don't worry, there won't be any problem. Our troops have rehearsed this type of manoeuvre many times before in Germany,"* answered Oberst Glaesemer.

On the signal, the Panzergrenadiere

DOCUMENTARY REPORT WITH THE S. PZ.ABT. 503

by Bild-Berichter Wolf-Allvater from PK 637
(Propaganda Company 637) (ECPAD DAT 3019)

Left: *The smoke and the dust from the explosions drift over the village while three women run for their lives from the planes. In the distance, the harbingers of death relentlessly carry on with their work of destruction.*
(© ECPAD DAT 3019- L24)

Top left: *In the heat of this village devastated by the air force, this messenger is not only bringing the mail but also a rabbit and a hen which will please the bellies of the 503rd. Survival first. Our Melder is wearing the rubberised raincoat designed originally for the motorbike riders. He has lowered his dust goggles and put them round his neck. He is wearing a black forage cap showing that he belongs to the armoured arm.*
(© ECPAD DAT 3019- L20)

Top right: *These Russian women are recovering whatever they can find that might be of use from among the debris caused by a bomb blast. Near them is the body of a Russian peasant who can be seen on another picture but not visible here. The planes caused severe damage before the reporter arrived. But it was not all over yet..*
(© ECPAD DAT 3019- L23)

Left: *This famous photograph shows the principal characters in this report. NCOs from 3./s. Pz.Abt. 503 listen to the Kdr., next to the air coordination officer wearing a white shirt. It is most likely that this man has called in the air force at the request of the 503rd to bomb the village before the Tigers get there. This shot shows several officers and NCOs who were identified later, Leutnant Weinert, Oberfähnrich Rondorf, Hauptfeldwebel Kiseberth. The Bild-Berichter was keen on putting Tiger 334 in the background in order to reinforce the impact of his photograph. The Melder's motorbike is also there, a Zundapp KS 750.*
(© ECPAD DAT 3019- L25)

above: *This shot shows us that this report was made just after an air raid. The houses in the village are still burning after the fighter-bombers and the Tigers have left it. This slice of life photographed by the reporter shows the daily life of the German soldiers and the civilians in Russia: a tragedy causing profound moral wounds and conflicts between notions of loyalty and the duty to obey, often well beyond normal personal convictions and a sense of honour.*
(© ECPAD DAT 3019- L28)

Below: *After being repaired several Tigers from 2./s. Pz.Abt. 503 attempted to join up with their CO who was waiting impatiently for them to arrive before launching an attack on Alexandrovka. But they were attacked on the way. Tiger 212 was hit and 232 caught fire. Seen here is 212, photographed by the Red Army. (Photo: DR)*
Another shot of Tiger 212. The tank seems only to have been hit in the rear as shown by the clearly visible impacts. (Photo: DR)

from I./Pz.Gren.Rgt.6 and II./Pz. Gren.Rgt.74 started off at a run, hurrying along the side of the woods on their left and then rushed at the Russians screaming. Neither of these battalions had SPWs. At the same time salvoes from the Werfer fell upon the Russians, petrifying them. The mortars spat out their shells at a terrifying rate. Explosions followed each other among the groups of Russian soldiers who were under pressure from all sides and suddenly found themselves completely disorganised. All the Kampfgruppe's forces were engaged in this battle which ended with bloody hand to hand fighting. A short while afterwards, Oberst Glaesemer sent a victory message to Generalmajor von Funck: *"We have broken the Russian attack. We have cost them about 400 men and we have captured about 200 of them. The 28th Guards Infantry Regiment doesn't exist any more!"*

"Well played, Herr Oberst!. We won't leave it at that. Get your Kampfgruppe together and join up with Oberleutnant Reuss' Pz. AA 7. The two of you will protect the army corps' flank. That is an order from Breith's HQ."

"This message is significant!" the adjutant replied to the Oberst, *"He's going to get us all killed, right down to the last man!"*

A short while later, a liaison officer arrived at Oberst Glaesemer's HQ. He opened his Meldetasche (map case) and took out a Russian map which he handed to the Oberst. The Oberst unfolded it and saw a big red line designating Kampfgruppe Glaesemer's front line beginning at Melikhovo and passing through Komintern finishing at Kasatzh. There was a message with the map. *"Stop the enemy here whatever the cost!"*

Oberst Glaesemer obeyed in spite of himself. He knew that his tactical group was not strong enough to hold off the Russians even though it had been reinforced by the divisional reconnaissance battalion. Gen. d. Pz. Tr. Breith's staff seemed to become aware of the fact because 168.I.D. came up to relieve them in the afternoon.

After spending a week being repaired at the rear, Gefreiter Günther Polzin's Tiger 224, together with other tanks from 2.Kp., tried to rejoin the last remaining Tigers in the Abteilung.

Unfortunately, Tiger 212 was hit on the way and 232 caught fire straight-away, although the crew did have the time to get out alive. Hünersdorff, Bohnhof, Kitzmann and Unteroffizier Koefling were wounded. Despite these incidents, on the evening of 13 July, Tiger 224 reached the commander of 2.Kp., Hauptmann Heilmann,

Oberst Friedrich-Carl von Steinkeller, Kdr. of Pz.Gren.Rgt.7 during the Battle of Kursk. He was born on 28 March 1896 at Deutsch Krone in East Prussia. After taking part in WWI, he entered the Reichswehr in which he was promoted quickly since he was a Major when war was declared. He was then put in command of the Kradschützen-battalion 2 (in 7. Pz.Div.) He led his unit to Toulon then was engaged in Russia where he was awarded the German Gold Cross in 1942. At the beginning of the following year, he was appointed Kdr. of Pz.Gren.Rgt.7. In March he was awarded the Knight's Cross. 1944 was decisive for his military career. He was made an Oberst then a Generalmajor. He was in command of the Feldherrnhalle Division when he was captured by the Russians on 8 July 1944. He only returned in 1955 from captivity.

Top right: **Oberst von Steinkeller in the company of Generalmajor Schulz.** (Photo: Coll. J. Charita)

who told Gefreiter Polzin that they were going to attack Alexandrovka the following morning, at 5 o'clock, with 7. Pz.Div.

It was a fact that the armoured units which had to attack in the morning had been battered about a bit before being able to reach their kick-off points. A report noted the reasons for the offensive being cancelled: terrain not adapted to Panzers, air activity and Russian artillery placed on the heights dominating the Donets.

At the end of the evening, 7. Pz.Div. was spread out along the Melikhovo-Schlachovozhe – Olkhovatka - Werchene Olschanez. line.

14 JULY 1943

During the night of 13-14 July 1943, the 53rd Armoured Guards Regiment and the 689th Anti-Tank Artillery Regiment joined up with the forces already present in front of Alexandrovka. The Russians were convinced that there was going to be another attack.

Generalmajor von Funck's staff had spent most of the night drawing up a new plan for capturing this small town. The organisation had been complete-

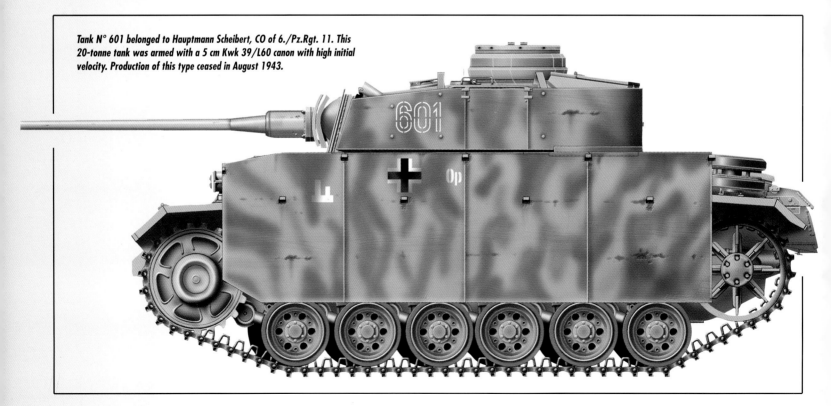

Tank N° 601 belonged to Hauptmann Scheibert, CO of 6./Pz.Rgt. 11. This 20-tonne tank was armed with a 5 cm Kwk 39/L60 canon with high initial velocity. Production of this type ceased in August 1943.

DOCUMENTARY REPORT WITH THE WERKSTATT
OF II./PZ.RGT. 11. *by Bild Berichter Helstaedt (DAT 3032-3034)*

Top left: *Major Bäke has installed his HQ in a wood. He is reading a report on the bravery of the Stabsgefreiter standing to attention in front of him. In a few moments he is going to ask the soldier to sign his deposition, requesting the regimental CO for a decoration. Then he is going to congratulate him and shake his hand. A tray will be brought forward and everybody will toast this soldier who is clearly moved by the ceremony. For this two pots of flowers have been placed on either side of the table so that Bäke's recommendation for an award will be placed between the two vases when the soldier signs it. German organisation is still meticulous, even in the middle of the Battle of Kursk. On Bäke's left, there is a tank section commander, a Feldwebel wearing the rush green canvas combat dress with chevrons. We can see two officers in combat dress from behind. On one of the other photographs in this report, one of them has been decorated with the Spanish Cross and is wearing a cap with dark Russian braid which recalls the colour of the artillery arm. (DAT 3032- L04)*

Top right: *While Major Bäke presides over the ceremony, the mechanics from the Werkstatt remove a turret from a Pz. III fitted with a 5-cm canon with the help of 4.5-tonne crane lorry of which only the hook system can be seen here. This is the tank belonging to the CO of 6./Pz.Rgt. 11, Hauptmann Scheibert. On the left of the side skirt, the position of the Balkenkreuz and the Op of Oppeln Bronowski are visible. This insignia was painted on the machines in his regiment between 18 February and 14 November 1943. (DAT 3032- L12)*

Right:
This Pz. IV Ausf G equipped with a 75-mm gun starting up did not escape the war correspondent's notice. Except for a Panzerschütze who is smiling at the photographer, his comrades are tense. Between 5 and 17 July, Bäke's armoured Abteilung lost three Flammenwerfers, nine Pz. IIIs and 13 Pz. IVs. It is interesting to note that out of eight crew members all wearing the black forage cap, two of them have insisted on keeping the pink braid of their arm, which was against regulations. (DAT 3032- L32)

Below: *After placing a plank (probably a piece of a casing from a lorry) over two fuel barrels, these two soldiers are using it as a work bench. They are putting 7.92 bullets into the belt with the help of a specially designed tool. The wide open shirt of the soldier smoking a pipe enables us to see his Erkennengsmarke (identity disc). Once again we can see the armoured unit's tactical sign and the Op above it, on the lorry. Unfortunately the filtering sun's rays do not allow us to see the company's number which would necessarily be on the right of the tactical sign.* (DAT 3032- L35)

Above:
The rear of this turret of a Pz. IV Ausf G has been hard hit. Looking more closely it seems that two enemy shells pierced the turret and came out the other side. The tactical insignia of 6. Pz.Div. with the Op above it shows us once again how the tanks in Bäke's Abteilung were painted. The mechanics have taken out various items from their lorries including a forge and a welding unit mounted on a chariot. All the more details for the pleasure of our more experienced modelists. (DAT 3032- L30)

Below:
One of the Pz. IIIs from 8./Pz.Rgt. 11 under Oberleutnant Spiekermann is also sheltering under the foliage. This is a Pz. III Ausf M or N. Sitting on an ammunition case wearing bathing trunks, a Panzerschütze is concentrating on his sewing watched by his comrade. Letters, a cardboard box, two small files and two bottles of ink have been placed on this makeshift table: a single plank placed on pieces of wood. (DAT 3034- L11)

Right:

This Panzer III Ausf D1 belonged to the HQ of II./Pz.Rgt.11 as indicated by the first number painted on the turret. It was armed with an MG 34 machine gun. The canon seen here is a dummy. Note the big antenna which distinguished it from the combat Pz. III. The armoured company tactical insignia seems to have been replaced by a white cross with the Op underneath, found on all the 6. Pz.Div. Armoured Abteilung machines. The white cross represents the divisional insignia worn by 6. Pz.Div. between January and April 1943. (DAT 3034- L17)

Middle:

Abteilung Bäke was specially equipped with 13 flame thrower tanks or Panzerkampfwagen III (Fl)s or even Sd Kfz 141/3s for the Battle of Kursk. Only 28 others were distributed to 11.Pz.Div. and to the Gross Deutschland. It was in fact a Pz. III to which the mechanics at the Wegmann factory had installed a flamethrower in place of the 5-cm KwK L/60 canon. Although the range of the flame's jet was limited to only 60 yards or so, it was an effective weapon for close quarter combat, supporting the infantry during attacks on trenches or clearing positions which were supposed to be impregnable. (DAT 3034- L12)

Below:

Hiding at the edge of the wood, this Pz. IV Ausf G from II./Pz.Rgt. 11 is ready to fire with its long 75-mm canon. As the Panther was not available at the end of 1942 and as the Russians had more powerful tanks, the Pz. IV was improved, particularly by lengthening the barrel of its canon. 841 of them were delivered a short time before the attack on Kursk. Although all the companies were not entirely equipped with Pz. IVs, they did receive some examples. (DAT 3034- L29)

DOCCUMENTARY REPPORT
WITH S. PZ.ABT. 503
by bild berichter
Wolf-Allvater from p.K. 637
(© ECPAD DAT 3013)

Left:
This tank commander is wearing anti-glare goggles which were also anti-dust goggles. These were usually issued to AA servers in the Luftwaffe and the Navy.
(© ECPAD DAT 3013- L9)

Bottom left:
The traces of the Tiger's large tracks (72.5 cm – 28 in) are clearly visible in this cereal field. In order to reduce the ever-present danger of mines, one tank was designated to open the way. The others followed it, strictly in its tracks.
(© ECPAD DAT 3013- L14)

Bottom right
The commander of the first Tiger talking with a woman probably in Russian. Many of the Panzerschützen in the 503rd had some knowledge of Russian. The Nazi flag in the foreground is a recognition flag for the Luftwaffe
(© ECPAD DAT 3013- L25)

Right: *This "Frontovik" is wearing the reversible camouflaged overcoat. He is armed with the classic PPSH 41 and is barded with offensive grenades.*
(DR Caption by M. Chaubiron)

ly reviewed. A new Kampfgruppe was set up under Oberst von Steinkeller now ordered to relieve Kampfgruppe Glaesemer who had repeatedly thrown his Panzergrenadiere into the attack, only to gain a few hundred yards. For the time being, it was obviously impossible to get hold of Hill 222.1 situated near Vipolsovka - Grasnozhe Snamzhe.

When Oberst von Steinkeller listened to Oberst Glaesemer describing the situation in which his tactical group found itself, he realised that something different had to be done if he was to take the heights. He decided to attack north-eastwards from the Kurakovka side to break the Russian resistance which was weaker in this sector. Once there was a breach, he would be in a position to take Hill 222.1

Major Bäke of II./Pz.Rgt. 11 was waiting desperately for the order to move. But the operation was put off until later because Kampfgruppe von Steinkeller's rush to Andreyevka had been slowed up. Von Steinkeller told his company commanders to fall back because in front of them was a very strong contingent of infantry reinforced by anti-tank guns.

While the Panzergrenadiere were digging their foxholes as quickly as possible an enemy tank vanguard ran into them. The Russians had decided to block any attacking movements in the direc-

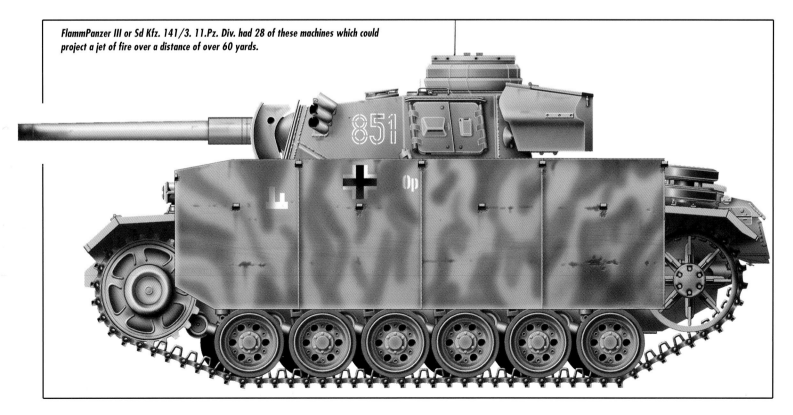

FlammPanzer III or Sd Kfz. 141/3. 11.Pz. Div. had 28 of these machines which could project a jet of fire over a distance of over 60 yards.

tion of Hill 222.1. The whole of the Kampfgruppe's strength was engaged in the front line. Oberst von Steinkeller insisted on taking part personally in the defensive fighting.

Suddenly on the right flank about thirty Russian tanks showed up. Fortunately the servers of three Paks which were particularly well-camouflaged opened fire. Three tanks were hit on the sides.

Oberst von Steinkeller noticed that the Russians hesitated.

"Get ready to intervene immediately!" he ordered his battalion commanders. What he wanted to do was to make the enemy think that he had strong reinforcements so that the Russians would fall back to their lines. The seven Russian tanks which wandered into range of the Paks were picked off immediately and destroyed.

On the signal, the Panzergrenadiere started shooting at the infantry who did not have time to fall back. Those who raised their arms were sent to the rear without accompanying guards.

The Russians got discouraged and broke off the fight. Their counter-attack was broken and their losses very heavy.

The CO of one of the three companies of Pz.Pi.Btl. 58, Oberleunant Ewald Baranek was awarded the Knight's Cross on 12 February 1943. Shortly afterwards he was given command of this engineers battalion which played such an important role in 7. Pz.Div. during the Battle of Kursk. (Photo J. Charita. Coll. D.L.)

Oberst von Steinkeller led his men on a new manoeuvre. This was to create a lot of the terrible summer dust on terrain which was not very suited for vehicles transporting troops quickly. Steinkeller even changed direction to get the Russians confused. His eyes screwed into his binoculars, he watched the slopes of Hill 222. 1 waiting for his Sappers to clear the mines. His Panzergrenadiere also waited anxiously for the passages through the minefield to be cleared so that they could capture this hill and have an end of it. With the irony of fate, it was Kampfgruppe Glaesemer (II./Pz.Gren.Rgt. 74 and I./Pz.Gren.Rgt. 6) in the end which took Hill 222.1. Luckily its scouts had spotted two suitable paths to the southwest of Vipolsovka which led them straight to their objective.

Generalmajor von Funck was directed by Gen. d. Pz. Tr. Breith to form two distinct groups. The first Kampfgruppe was to head west to join up with 2.SS-Pz.Div. Das Reich from II.SS-Pz.Korps - a total of 80 miles to be covered deep behind enemy lines! The second group had to take Alexandrovka as already ordered.

The only photograph showing Hauptmann Heilmann's Tiger 200 in 2./s. Pz.Abt. 503. The Grenadiers are moving up into the line. (© ECPAD DAT 3022- L3)

Above: *This BA 10 armoured car recognisable by the shape of its semi-circular hatch, the B 6's being square.* (DR Caption by M. Chaubiron)

Hauptmann von Kageneck assembled his eight last remaining operational Tigers in the battalion to lead the attack with the 20 Panzers of Major Bäke's II./Pz.Rgt. 11. But he was worried. Other Tigers from the Abteilung ought already to have joined up with them, but none of them had arrived yet.

Yet Günther Polzin from 2./s. Pz.Abt. 503 was desperately trying to get there on time with his Tiger to take part in the attack. *"We were almost alone"*, he recalled after the war *"and we soon had trouble with our sprocket wheels which broke down. The situation became critical because we had to be towed away under fire from the Russians. Our Tiger was hit 14 times. It was only during the evening that an Unteroffizier came to our rescue. We lost seven comrades:*

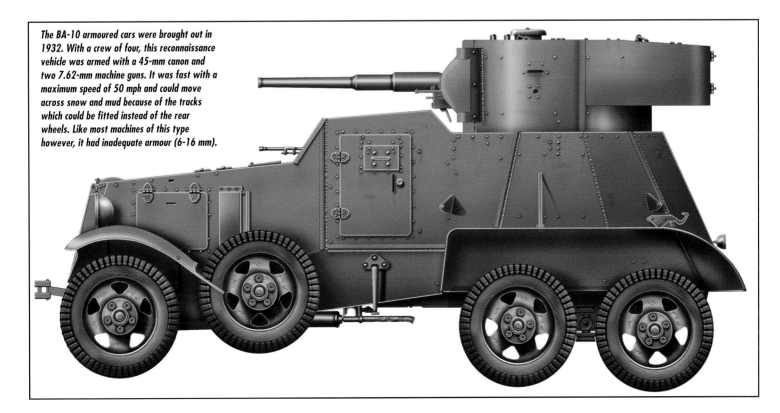

The BA-10 armoured cars were brought out in 1932. With a crew of four, this reconnaissance vehicle was armed with a 45-mm canon and two 7.62-mm machine guns. It was fast with a maximum speed of 50 mph and could move across snow and mud because of the tracks which could be fitted instead of the rear wheels. Like most machines of this type however, it had inadequate armour (6-16 mm).

Left:
Gefreiter Heinz Kühl's grave informs us that he belonged to the Stabskompanie of s. Pz.Abt. 503 and that he was killed on 21 July 1943. This BA 22/2948 report dates back to this period or during the following days. The scene is near the Smelok Trudu Redin sector. Gefreiter H. Kühl had still not been relieved. (BA 22/2948/19)

Next page top left: *After leaving Tiger 334, the reporter photographed one of the three section commanders of 1./s. Pz.Abt. 503. The driver is wearing the Heer's Feldgrau with pink bordered shoulder flaps and the Leutnant has kept his tankman's black uniform.* (BA 22/2948/9)

Next page middle left: *An ammunition supply lorry has just arrived. The five crew members get busy. Indeed in the morning of 22 July 1943, they were engaged with their comrades and destroyed ten T-34s. Wolfgang Schneider, the undisputed expert on Tiger units, states that these tanks destroyed seven other T-34s during the afternoon near Bishovka.* (BA 22/2948/22)

Next page right: *After rolling their sleeves up, the crew of 123 hand the shells up to be stored away in the tank; between 66 and 78 88-mm shells could be stowed away. There were two types of shells for the Tiger: the 92 Pz. Gr. and the 4,800 Patr. Smk. Spgr.* (BA 22/2948/24)

Next page bottom: *Standing inside the Tiger, the loader has opened his hatch and takes the shell in turn. He then passes it to the fifth member of the crew who stows it away on the rack. Note the bags of MG 34 ammunition belts.* (BA 22/2948/28)

Below: *The crew from Tiger 334 is repairing the tracks. The tanks often went over mines, which blew off one or more links in the track causing the tank to drive "off" its tracks. One of the wheels has been released on the left side in order to make the repairs easier. Because there were no means of towing it, Tiger 334 was scuttled by its crew on 13 September 1943 near Yefremovka.* (BA 22/2948/5)

Above: *One of the Panzerschützen preparing sandwiches for his mates who are busy loading the shells. At the end of 22 July, six Tigers were attached to Panzergruppe Bäke to take part in the counter-attack whose objective was to capture Hill 224.3 near Gorki where several T-34s were destroyed. Between 22-23 July 1943, three Tigers were lost.* (BA 22/2948/30)

Top right : *A Panzerschütze is filling up the water flasks with the help of a container used for that purpose. That is why there is a white cross painted on it. Note the civilian waistcoat worn by the soldier in the background.* (BA 22/2948/33)

Hans-Jürgen Burmester was born on 11 June 1916 in Lamstedt. After passing his school exams, he entered the Wehrmacht in 1935. He quickly became an officer in the anti-tank signals arm. He continued to serve with this rank during the Polish, Dutch and French campaigns. He then went to tank school where he remained until the beginning of 1942. Then he left for the Eastern front; he became 1./s. Pz.Abt. 503's CO and replaced the Tiger Battalion Commander several times. Transferred to s. Pz.Abt. 509, Burmester took part in the retreat from the Ukraine and was heavily engaged in the crossing of the Bug in June 1944. For his courage and devotion, he was awarded the Knight's Cross and promoted to Major. He only entered the Bundeswehr in 1956. He was decorated by President Heinemann with the Bundesverdienstkreuz. (Photo J. Charita. Coll. D.L.)

The Tiger crew from 1./s. Pz.Abt. 503 is busy maintaining their tank. Note that the tank's number has been painted on the Kanister. As for the company commander, Hauptmann Burmester (centre, wearing the Feldmütze), he is talking to Unteroffizier Lewandowski (foreground, right). On Burmester's left is Hauptfeldwebel Haase. When this report was made, Hauptmann Burmester had replaced Hauptmann von Kageneck who was convalescing. (BA 22/2948/36)

After unloading several crates of shells from a lorry which has come up to supply them, the Panzerschützen take a break. The next few days were going to be terrible because as at 31 August, s. Pz.Abt. 503 was reduced to just nine operational Tigers. (BA 22/2948/38)

five were wounded and two were killed, Reich and Unteroffizier Rump."

Amid the infernal cacophony of engines and explosions, Hauptmann von Kageneck once more launched his troops against Alexandrovka. The remnants of the Panzergrenadiere companies covered Major Bäke's last panzers.

The first line of defence was very quickly swept aside by the shells from the Pz. IV's 75-mms and the Tigers' 88-mm guns. The Russian positions were cleared out as much by the fire from the tanks as from the machine guns whose barrels were red-hot.

Suddenly Russian tanks appeared and a Very rocket soared into the sky. Major Bäke understood that his tanks had perhaps driven too far behind the enemy lines and that he would not be able to get any reinforcements if his luck turned against him. The shells from the Russian tanks bounced off the Tigers' armour but did not stop them in their mad dash. They rushed forward just as fast as their engines would take them and their merciless 88-mm canon got a direct hit each time they fired.

For one unending hour during which the Panzerschützen's nerves were on edge, they had the better of the Russian tanks which were no more than metal coffins in which their crew burned to death. To the cloud of black smoke which escaped from the wrecks was added the smell of oil, cordite and grilled human flesh.

After the tanks, the Panzerschützen had to deal with the Russian anti-tank guns. The Tiger Panzerschützen who had been asked to save on their ammunition consumption now were ordered to do exactly the opposite by their Kdr. *"Fire at will at the anti-tank guns!"*

The shells found new victims in the deafening racket. All the anti-tank gun positions caught fire and their guns fell silent one after the other.

A short while later, the infantry rushed towards the anti-tank ditch, the last Russian defence in front of the town the Panzerruppe Bäke soldiers could see the first roofs of. The assault Sappers intervened under the protection of the Panzergrenadiere. In record time, they opened up a suitable way through for the Panzers, then sent a radio message to Bäke and to von Kageneck to confirm that it was possible now to cross this obstacle.

Coming from the southeast, the Landsers of Gren. Rgt. 229 also attacked with the support of III. Pz.Korps' artillery. It was 8 a.m. when Gen. d. Pz. Tr. Breith's HQ received a message from Major Bäke, announcing that Alexandrovka had been captured.

During the engagement with the 53rd Armoured Guards Regiment, s. Pz.Abt. 503 destroyed 36 T-34s to take Alexandrovka. This large number of tanks destroyed by the crews of the Tiger battalion cannot be explained solely by the skill of these men and the Tiger's superiority alone, but also by the weakness of the Russian tanks themselves which had difficulty firing on the move and from a long range.

Pz.Rgt. 11's log records that a large number of prisoners were captured, that six T-34s and five T60s were destroyed, not counting the huge number of infantry weapons also destroyed.

Losses however were also recorded on the German side, Hauptmann Heilmann, CO of 2./s. Pz.Abt. 503., to mention but one. He was wounded, as were two others in his company.

Hauptmann Graf von Kageneck has left a record of one of the last engagements his unit took part in during Operation Citadel. Considering the number of Tigers which he says were in his unit, the fight seems to correspond with the fight for Alexandrovka. *"As we were always ahead it was our role to play the frontline watch dogs. Our neighbouring units fell back under pressure and Ivan advanced with powerful armoured forces. During one of these actions, I got together eight Tigers. Suddenly we were attacked while we were crossing a marshy sector. Behind there was an escarpment leading to higher ground. When we got there we found a awful sight. Infantrymen from a neighbouring unit were falling back in disorder while Russian tanks were moving among them mowing them down ruthlessly on all sides.*

We were had the advantage because those tanks were sitting ducks. In no time we had destroyed 20 of them. Once again the weaknesses of the T-34 were made evident. As the Russian tank commanders could not see anything around them from their turrets,

Tiger 212 was damaged and repaired but was attacked and hit in the rear as it was rejoining its unit. It caught fire and had to be abandoned.

The Kdr. of s. Pz.Abt. 503's Tiger I with its particular markings on the turret. At the time this photograph was taken, Hauptmann von Kageneck was convalescing. The Panzerschütze who is next to the turret is holding a little white parachute, or rather the contents of a signals cartridge shot by a Signals Pistole. (© ECPAD DAT 3020- L30)

they could not see that the tanks next to them were on fire. Then new targets appeared."

In the evening Panzerkampfgruppe Bäke set up a defensive line then headed west and the Panzerschützen were given permission to withdraw for two days.

Although the bad weather had delayed Oberstleutnant Schulz's tanks in their advance, his men fought with abnegation to join up with I2.SS-Pz.Div. Das Reich in the Mal Jablonovo sector. They reached the first units at around midday. In the beginning of the evening, they occupied Schlachovozhe then set up a bridgehead and then impatiently waited for reinforcements. Pz.Pi.Btl. 58 and II./Pz.Gren.Rgt. 7 followed by Kampfgruppe von Steinkeller eventually joined with them during the night.

Major Bäke performed a real miracle but at what price! 40 of his Panzers were left on the battlefield according to the official sources. This would appear to be excessive given the number of operational tanks his unit had at the beginning of the day. The number put forward seems to suggest more likely that the remnants of Pz.Rgt. 27 and StuG.Abt. 228 must have been engaged with Pz.Rgt. 25, for such a number to be reached. Once again, it is clear that the

The Tiger I was a command tank, witness the umbrella antenna. This tank belonged to the Kdr. of 2./s. Pz.Abt. 503, Hauptmann von Kageneck.

Above:

Nurses come to pay their last respects to General von Hünersdorff and say some words. It is quite probable that the General's wife was among them. She finished her speech by asking the officers and soldiers to remember the General with respect. Frau von Hünersdorff was a nurse at Karkhov Hospital during the summer of 1943. Among the patients she had to look after was a Leutnant von Rosen. (BA 22/2940/22)

KTB were not accurate enough and that they restricted themselves to reporting the actions only of the division concerned. The role neighbouring units played was mostly left out which leads one to one suppose that the hits claimed in the KTB were attributable only to the division concerned. In short the other divisions were relegated to a secondary role. Thus the part played by the three Tiger companies from s. Pz.Abt. 503 is rarely described in the marching logs of the 6., 7. and 19. Pz.Div. and even of III. Pz.Korps itself. As for StuG.Abt. 228, it almost as though it did not exist, event though it was present from the first to the last day of the operation.

The following day, Generalfeldmarschall von Manstein received an order from the Führer's headquarters. He was to withdraw II.SS-Pz.Korps from the front and transfer it to the west of Belgorod. XXXXVIII Pz. Korps would relieve it and 3./SS-Pz.Div. *Totenkopf* would be attached to it.

This spelt the end of Operation Citadel. Heeresgruppe Sud under Generalfeldmarschall von Manstein now entered a defensive phase, or even the beginning of a withdrawal.

The veteran and ex-Kdr. of s. Pz.Abt. 503, Hauptmann von Kageneck evokes this period of retreat towards the south:

"There was nothing left to do but withdraw. Few orders from high command came down to us. We were practically alone on the left flank just as much as we were on the right. As long as there was daylight we advanced across the steppes here and there. During the night we had to be watchful because we no longer had the infantry in support. This was a new experience for our crews. My tank was in position on the right of the road (...)

" Finally the following morning I got into touch by radio with 7. Pz.Div. I advised them that I still had some Tigers and that the enemy was increasing the pressure. Our force covered about three miles to the south.

"When one of our tanks was put out of action by a hit straight to the gearbox, I went off to help the crew.

"All around us the steppe was buzzing with Russians. The anti-tank guns were still invisible.

"When I was about ten yards from the other Tiger, I gave the signal from my turret to the crew that had to be rescued, to come over and join me. It was at this very moment that I was hit on the hand and the forearm by shrapnel. I lost consciousness and fell. I remained lying for about an hour on the side of the road. Suddenly a general asked me some questions energetically about the situation at the front. I opened my eyes but all I could see was red and gold coloured spots.

"Three days later, at Karkhov hospital, I found Smend, the adjutant who was rescued by the crew of another tank. I learnt that thanks to him, the rest of the Abteilung reached our lines. There was no doubt that the fighting we took part in quite considerably influenced the overall operations. That is why Gen. d. Pz. Tr. Breith put me up for the Knight's Cross.

"Later, my headquarters found itself in the Snarmenka sector and I was furious to learn that the Army Corps General, General Stemmermann had assigned each of my three companies to one of his three divisions. He must have been thinking of one of Goebbels' speeches which said 'where there is a Tiger, the enemy does get through.' His words of course were much more optimistic than those, much wiser, from General Guderian, who said: 'Never skimp, always pull out all the stops.'

"I was in a hurry to reach the next HQ situated about 20 miles away at Kirovograd. It was General Wöhler's, of the 8. Armee. I was received by a Chief-of-Staff who seemed to me to be more of a philosopher than a person of some importance.

"It was then that I met General Speidel; I told him about my situation and my opinion concerning the fundamental way of engaging Tigers. I quic-

kly discovered that he agreed with me.

"Three days later, my three Tiger companies were together again at Snamenka. That day, the Russian armour attacked the bridgehead to the east of the Dniepr and overran General Stemmermann's HQ. We saw all his staff and the General in person retreating in full flight. Our reunited Tigers clarified the situation by launching an immediate counter-attack. We got things to calm down in our sector."

During the evening of 16 July, the last six Panzers in Pz.Rgt. 11 gave up any hope of obtaining the victory for which they had fought so hard and headed south where they passed their old battlefields, this time going in the opposite direction.

The following day, the Kdr. of their division, Generalmajor von Hunersdorff died of his wounds. His wife was pre-

Above: *The funeral of General von Hünersdor f* (BA 22/2940/18)

sent at the funeral and addressed the following words to the soldiers in his division: "Remember your general with respect."

This sentence could also be applied to the 1 271 German soldiers in III. Pz.Korps who fell during Operation Citadel.

Below: *With his Field Marshall's baton, for the last time von Manstein salutes one of the greatest armoured unit commanders the army had ever had known.* (BA 22/2940/24)

CONCLUSION ABOUT THE MANNER IN WHICH III. PZ.KORPS WAS USED DURING THE BATTLE OF KURSK.

REPORT ON LOSSES AND STATISTICS

The official document from the Inspector-General of Armoured Troops established minimal losses for the tanks, which disagreed totally with the veterans' eye-witness accounts and the unit log books. For instance if the number of Panzers remaining as at 15 July in Pz.Rgt. 11 are taken into consideration, it could only line up only six tanks whereas the official document mentions a total of only 25 tanks destroyed as at 17 July 1943. Could there therefore have been more than six tanks fit for battle on 15 July?

According to another German document, only 190 Panzers or Sturmgeschütze from Army Group South were destroyed during the whole operation. This same document gives 25 Panzers destroyed for Pz.Rgt. 11, 10 Panzers for Pz.Rgt. 25, 27 for Pz.Rgt. 27, three Tigers for s. Pz.Abt. 503 and one single Strumgeschutz for StuG.Abt. 228. In all 66 tanks lost between 5 and 17 July 1943 for III. Pz.Korps.

However this may be, all the KTBs agree that the total number of operational tanks as at 13 July for III. Pz.Korps was 63 tanks, or almost 14% of the total number of tanks available compared with its initial strength.

This difference can be explained by the fact that the workshops worked miracles. All are agreed on this point. In a single day's work, the mechanics were able to repair a large number of tanks. A convincing example would be the case of Pz. Brigade 10 which, out of 200 Panthers engaged on 5 July only had 12 operational tanks on the 9th, then received 33 others from the repair workshops, increasing therefore the number of operational tanks to 44 (one of them was lost in the meantime).

It must therefore be admitted that German losses as far as equipment was concerned during the Battle of Kursk were far from being catastrophic since only 12.5% of the forces engaged were lost, or very precisely 190 tanks out of the 1 508 belonging to Army Group South!

Russian losses are easier to determine in the sector covered by III. Pz.Korps because they are known from the Russian sources; 1 571 tanks were destroyed between 5 and 24 July, on the Voronezh front alone, a similar figure to the one put forward by the German archives. Taking as a basis the losses suffered by this army corps compared with Army Group South, it can be estimated that between 500 and 550 Russian tanks were lost in the III. Pz.Korps sector. In other words a third of the Russian armoured forces was destroyed by each of the three German armoured corps engaged in the south.

By comparing the figures of the two belligerents in the sector where General Breith's forces were engaged, 7 Russian tanks were lost for every German Panzer.

Day by day strength of the Armoured Forces according to III. Pz.Korps Headquarters

6. Pz.Div. :
- 67 panzers on 9 july
- 22 panzers on 10 july
- 12 panzers on 12 july

7. Pz.Div. :
- 36 panzers on 9 july
- 43 panzers on 10 july
- 50 panzers on 11 july
- 36 panzers on 12 july

19. Pz.Div. :
- 35 panzers on 9 july.
- 12 panzers on 10 july
- 14 panzers on 11july
- 11 panzers on 12 july

s. Pz.Abt. 503 :
- 33 Tigeron 9 july
- 14 Tiger on 10 july
- 23 Tiger on 11 july

Stg.Abt. 228 :
- 23 Stg.on 9 july
- 11 Stg. on 10 july
- 19 Stg. on 12 july

The Panzers lost were lost for the following reasons:
60% - anti-tank guns
5% - engagements with other tanks
5% - mines
5% - getting stuck
6% - enemy artillery

According to the documents from KTB AOK 8 the losses of each of the divisions attached to III. Pz.Korps were the following for the period 4 July to 20 July 1943.

Division	Killed	Wounded	Missing	total
6. Pz.Div.	273	1 523	25	1 821
7. Pz.Div.	235	1 219	33	1 487
19. Pz.Div.	266	1 758	94	2 118
168. I.D.	420	2 132	71	2 623
Corps units	27	140	0	167
Total	1 221	6 772	223	8 216

CONTENTS

ACKNOWLEDGEMENTS AND THANKS

After his invaluable help with my book "*45 Tigers in Normandy*", I would like to thank once again Generalmajor von Rosen for his precious eye-witness account of Operation Citadel, as well as the Kameradschaft of s. Pz.Abt. 503 which handed over the unit's archives to me.
My thanks extend to Raoul Mantulak, Jan-Hendrik Wendler, Tomsov Alexandr Sergeievitch and Marko Vidmar who constantly supported me through the Axis History forum (http:/forum. Axishistory.com). Thanks also to Thierry Guilbert for his usual help as well as to the members of the forum Croixdefer.com for their encouragement. Finally my thanks also to Jean-Luc Leleu and Alain Verwicht for their enlightened opinion on certain obscure points; without forgetting Joseph Charita, Laurent Huard, Claude Langlois, Mathieu Hanot and Pierre Tiquet.
To Jean Mabire for his work.

Biblography :

- Archives Kameradschaft de la s. Pz.Abt. 503.
- KTB 7. Pz.Div. RH 27-6
- KTB 6. Pz.Div. RH 27-7
- KTB 19. Pz.Div. RH 27-19
- KTB III.Pz.Korps - RH 24-3
- Brennpunkte - Wolfgang Paul
- 19. Infanterie und Panzer-Division - Rolf Hinze
- Koursk 1943 - Niklas Zetterling and Anders Frankson
- The battle for Koursk - The Soviet General Staff Study
- Traditionsverband ehem. 7. Panzer-Division
- "Panzer Voran" by Alan Verwicht. For all those interested in the study of German units, I strongly recommend this review which is essential reading and richly illustrated.

By the same author : (in french)

- "45 Tigers en Normandie" (45 Tigers in Normandy): History and analysis of s. Pz.Abt. 503's participation fighting the Battle of Normandy.
- "Objectif Chambois": The US 90th Inf. Div. participation in closing the Falaise Gap.
- "D'Argentan à la Seine" (From Argentan to the Seine) the Panther Battalion of 19. Pz.Div. to the end of August 1944.
- "La Massue" (The Bludgeon) The odyssey of the 1st Polish Armoured Division during the Battle of Normandy, from Operation Totalize to the closing of the Falaise Gap.
- "Combats sur la Seine" (Fighting on the Seine), Vol. I: the odyssey of 17. FeldDiv. (L) at the end of the Battle of Normandy.
- "La Division Meindl" ("the Meindl Division"), the history of the first Jäger unit realised with help the Veterans Association "Der Adler".
http://didierlodieu.site.voila.fr

Editing by Denis Gandilhon.
Design and lay-out by Antoine Poggioli and Gil Bourdeaux.
Drawing by Nicolas Gohin.
© Histoire & Collections 2007

Histoire & Collections
SA au capital de 182 938, 82 €

5, avenue de la République
F-75541 Paris Cédex
11 FRANCE

Tel: 00 33 1 40 21 18 20
Fax: 00 33 1 47 00 51 11

www.histoireetcollections.fr

This book has been designed, typed, laid-out and processed by *Histoire & Collections* and *Le Studio Graphique A&C*, fully on integrated computer equipment. Color separation by *Le Studio Graphique A&C*

Printed by ZURE, Spain, European Union.
February 2007